WILLIAM LANGLAND

MEDIEVAL AND RENAISSANCE AUTHORS

General Editors

John Norton-Smith

*Professor of English
University of Dundee*

Douglas Gray

*J. R. R. Tolkien Professor of English
Literature and Language
University of Oxford*

Volume 6

William Langland

JOHN NORTON-SMITH

LEIDEN — E. J. BRILL — 1983

ISBN 90 04 06932 1

PRINTED IN THE NETHERLANDS

In Memoriam
Robert Browning
d. 19 October 1964

Yet it may be that there is a zone of silence in the
middle of every art. The artists themselves live in
it.

CONTENTS

PREFACE

In writing this study of William Langland I have tried to remember the injunction of Virginia Woolf: 'Do not dictate to your author; try to become him. Be his fellow-worker and accomplice.' Yet, as she later admits in the same essay, the gifted author remains, for all our close manoeuverings, irresistibly himself. We often begin in intended sympathy only to end in admiration (however qualified) of the otherness, surprising and enlarging, of the experience of another mind whose often elusive identity remains unassimilatible to our own. The reader of this study will have to endure that paradox and will have to make allowance for my early training at the hands of two tutors and close friends, C. S. Lewis and J. A. W. Bennett, who communicated their satisfaction and dissatisfaction with the poet and his much revised poem. Evidence of a mixture of sympathies and critical reservations will be detected in my own response to Langland.

I am grateful for the generous help and criticism of the General Editor of this series, Professor Douglas Gray. I thank Mr Edward Wilson, Fellow of Worcester College, Oxford for all his guidance and correction. Finally, I must thank Moira Anthony for her skill and patience in preparing the typescript. I am grateful to the Bodleian Library, Oxford, for permission to quote from MS Laud Misc. 581.

Glencairn,
Newport-on-Tay, Fife.
6 December 1981

ABBREVIATIONS

EC	*Essays in Criticism*
ELH	*English Literary History*
MAE	*Medium Aevum*
MED	*Middle English Dictionary*
MP	*Modern Philology*
ME	Middle English
OE	Old English
OED	*Oxford English Dictionary*
OF	Old French
PBA	*Proceedings of the British Academy*
RES	*The Review of English Studies*

Line references in quotations from *Piers Plowman* are to: Prologue—Passus VII, *Langland: Piers Plowman,* ed. J. A. W. Bennett, Oxford (1972); Passus VIII-XX, *The vision of William concerning Piers the Plowman,* ed. W. W. Skeat, Oxford, (1886), Vol. I. Folio references are to Bodley MS. Laud Misc. 581 which forms the basis of the text used in this book.

CHAPTER ONE

Introduction

Awakened by the cock-crow—(a sermon, a sickbed or a providen-
tial escape)—the Christian pilgrim sets out in the morning twilight
while yet the truth (the νόμος τέλειος ὁ τῆς ἐλευθερίας) is below the
horizon. Certain necessary consequences of his past life and his
present undertaking will be seen by the refraction of its light: more
will be apprehended and conjectured. The phantasms, that had
predominated during the long hours of darkness, are still busy.
Though they no longer present themselves as distinct forms, they
yet remain as formative notions in the pilgrim's soul, unconscious
of its own activity and over-mastered by its own workmanship.
Things take the signature of thought. The shapes of the recent
dream become a mould for the objects in the distance and these
again give an outwardness and sensation of reality to the shaping
of the dream.

S. T. Coleridge, Aids to Reflection, Aphorism xxix.

The poet Chaucer perhaps only once approaches the devotional intensity and special spirituality of Langland when portraying Christ
crucified. The passage does not occur in the *ABC* nor do we find it in
that 'miracle' which was to provide the origins of Lydgate's style for
the interminable *Lyf of Our Lady*. The moment occurs in the simple
stanzaic fable-style designed for the *Man of Law's Tale*; it appears at a
moment of crisis in the much-tested life of Constance at the point
when she is about to board ship, when she fears death by drowning:

> 'O cleere, o welful auter, holy croys,
> Reed of the Lambes blood ful of pitee,
> That wessh the world fro the olde iniquitee,
> Me fro the feend and fro his clawes kepe,
> That day that I shall drenchen in the depe.
>
> Victorious tree, proteccioun of trewe,
> That oonly worthy were for to bere

The Kyng of Hevene with his woundes newe,
The White Lamb, that hurt was with a spere,
Flemere of feendes out of hym and here,
On which thy lymes feythfully extenden,
Me kepe, and yif me myght my lyf t'amenden.'

(*CT*.B 450-462)

In Constance's prayer we glimpse the potency of the blood which flows down to nourish the 'plante of pes' which in its turn is strengthened by the earth which bears it—the heart-piercing process of suffering through which Christ became the *Redemptor*. Constance's intensity of feeling immediately recalls Langland more than it does the phraseology of Fortunatus. The context is at once full of the emotional actuality of Constance's terror yet at the same time the experience is transmitted to us in a verbal style which is deliberately unsophisticated and does not aim at reproducing experience by means of whatever 'naturalism' medieval poetics was capable of. The contrast between the local moment of vividness, of the energy of a real situation, and the simple, story-telling style is deliberate on Chaucer's part—just as the affective ending of the tale, the romantic recognition scene and justified reconcilement miraculously survive the simplied artifice of the 'story' and its arguably wearisome 'testing' framework. Something like this contrast is attempted by Shakespeare in *Pericles* and *The Winter's Tale*. This kind of formal invention represents a sophisticated author's cultivation of archaistic and simple forms and styles which defy the audience to believe in them, and then, by the subtle manipulation of local moments of genuine pathos and faithful rendering of actual experience, defy us to disbelieve in them. No wonder that Shakespeare openly attributes the workmanship of Hermione's statue to 'Julio Romano' (the only Renaissance artist ever named by Shakespeare). The reference in Paulina's attribution is to Giulio Romano's brilliant *trompe l'oeil* effects in painting: where the relation between art and nature amounts to deception, openly connived at. The viewer's response which arises out of the sheer technical manipulation of artistry is one of wonder and enchantment.[1] The theatre-goer responds similarly, and the same response, I believe, is aroused by the form and style of the *Man of Law's Tale*. Chaucer achieves this result through a sophisticated application of his mastery of the art of poetry.

By contrast, Langland's technical proficiency and literary training seem less assured, and sometimes have been esteemed defective or inadequate. His poem triumphantly achieves three moments, crowning moments, of Christocentric force in one literary dimension, and, equally, on another plane he images forth satiric renderings of contemporary society which create an impression of reality with immediate, short-hand, expressiveness. These are distinctive and impressive achievements. But the general level of Langland's verse writing, the proliferation of the digressive, the long leading-up to set-pieces, and the unsustained movement of the whole *narratio* fail to provide an adequate artistic milieu for the climaxes and the crucial 'recognition scenes'. What is simplistic and 'unsophisticated' in Langland's poetic technique is not the result of a calculating artistry but comes about through a lack of it. Further, most artists (with few exceptions) acknowledge the innate limitations of mimesis. The formal power of art can create the impression of truth, an imitation of a certain reality, but that same shaping force cannot embody or endlessly recreate the original situation of reality. There is a point where mimesis not only stops, but where formal imitation reveals its genuine opposite nature—its artificiality, its 'artefactness'—if the coinage may be allowed. Langland, when compared with Chaucer, seems to have this fundamental aesthetic paradox a little out-of-focus. At one point, in his exchange with Imaginatyf, the poet-dreamer gives the detailed impression (by way of justifying his writing of verses—the citing of 'Cato' is in itself reductive) that poetic composition is merely recreative, hardly serious enough for morality or living, yet everywhere Langland the poet is determined to pour his dreamer's experience red-hot into the cold mould of his own lines. The garrulousness, encircling and threatening to overwhelm the main drift of the argument, reminds us of later egoists, Browning, Whitman and Pound—poets who fancied themselves as authenticating historians of large scenes and great gulfs of time and space. Here the literary critic must face the problems raised by the nature of the historical consciousness of the artist who attempts such ambitious sweeps of time. Of the three modern poets just mentioned, one could argue that Browning was probably the most scholarly and best-informed as to the authenticity and the effective uses of historical research and knowledge. Yet the lasting impression of the longer, more complex historical poems (the *Ring and the Book* apart) is that he was drawn to using 'history' in a mystifying and recondite vein— a

vein which seems a little too self-regarding and often not a little boring. Pound's reading of 'history' (the index to the *Guide to Kulcher*
makes a strange inventory) is plainly pedantic, the messianic voice
always blending with the hermetic and urgent whisper of a strange
scholarship: inside information gathered from obscure texts,
marginalia and bibliographies. For Whitman, 'history' seems to have
been made up of its grander, popular narratives, a journalistic
reading of past achievements and experience touched by a diverted,
crusading ardour. Of course, Langland as an 'historian' cannot be
compared *tout simple* with any of these poets. His sense of 'history'
(and his 'texts') is not theirs. But even by the best educated standards
of the fourteenth century, he seems to show little or no reading
knowledge of any reputable historian nor to have properly grasped
the working-method of any single style of historiography. What
would he have made of John of Salisbury much less Livy or
Suetonius? Not much, one is tempted to surmise. As a poet-historian
of the development and functioning of medieval social institutions he
appears to have had no reading models and little or no working principles, unless one sees his critical aim as an educationalization of life
itself, as if his chief guiding principle had been extracted from one of
his favourite fundamental texts, the *Disticha Catonis* (III.i.):

> Instrue praeceptis animum, ne discere cessa,
>   nam sine doctrina vita est quasi mortis imago.
> (Cease not to learn, equip your mind with rules,
>   for without rules and precepts life is a picture of death).

The last chapter of this present study (pp. 123-131) will attempt to
show how thorough-going was Langland's devotion to the 'educationalization of life itself'.

Langland is little better as an ecclesiastical historian, as far as he
allows us to judge. His habitual appreciation of the historical process
seems to be one of viewing synchronically in so far as the results are
reflected in contemporary practice. And this contemporary practice is
judged morally on the social results achieved and how faithfully the
practice is modelled on the theory or idea from which 'practice' is
opined to have originated. Essence precedes existence as far as social
institutions are concerned in Langland's historical analysis. The
behaviour of knights or clergy or any other 'estate' is determined by
the theoretical function for which it was morally designed. Langland
seems unaware that such a type of definition might amount to a ra-

tionalization. The close connection between function and 'ideal' tends to eliminate the complex historical analysis of any interplay between human activity and political ideas in any passage of the poem. The fundamentalist in Langland is strong and single-minded. Restoration comprises Langland's habitual mode of 'reform', for historical or temporal evolution is a sequence unrepresented in the poet's social analysis—unless it is exemplified by the sequence of decay or perversion. The poet can imagine perversion as an historical cause or sequence as accomplished by the individual or collective *voluntas*. He seems not to be able to imagine any other more complicated process, especially any historical sequence free from moral intention. Accidents (including natural disasters) seldom if ever occur. Thus, Langland's account of the coming into being and functioning of his own institutions has no natural perspective or sense of neo-classical dimensions of 'theory' or 'practice'—or none of the Dantean interpretation of ages, prophecy or historical evolution. Prophecy as 'history' is understood by Langland but darkly and according to popular usage. The tone of the poet's inquiry is coloured by the exemplary and the epideictic in a spirit alien to Dante as well as Aristotle. All this historical 'monodimensionalism' gives an air or urgency to the author's questionings but his inquisition's discreteness or accuracy cannot be tested. The evidence has been by-passed by the theoretical purity of the method—how the evidence became 'evidence' in the first place.

It is not difficult to see how Langland, in common with other minds of the period, came to imagine that the hieratic origins of medieval society (so strongly influenced by the categorizing tendencies of the Pseudo-Dionysius and the political and theological syntheses of patristic explanations and rationalizations) would substantially contain a recoverable unity of social and philosophical expression, recoverable and therefore capable of revitalisation through man's obedience to the theoretical 'harmonies' advanced by the system, especially man's participation in the doctrine of common use and his performance of good works. This altruistic application of human energy would be sufficient to revitalize the existing political and social forms of 'government' which had only in a very small part emerged from theory and dogma, but in reality had evolved from an entirely different and far less 'altruistic' mixture of ideas, baser acquisitive forces, will to power, together with all the complications of statecraft, deceptions, intrigues, inter-estate extortion, or mere evolving practical experience. But the gap between perfectible model and the actual ramshackle bastardized organisations of late medieval feudality was not only too great, but the organizations never in the first place emerged from a coherent intention (much less grand design) of historical or philosophical realization. Self-interest and a bewildering variety of 'interests' had been and were still at work producing the temporal unfolding of this society and its possible and impossible goals and ideals. The semi-feudal social structure and the great political powers (temporal and spiritual) which Langland found himself faced with were the result of a complex interplay of responses to events which would require an entirely different sort of intelligence to analyse all these often incompatible expressions of theory and practice. Reconciliation and 'harmonization' of the incompatibilities at the time seemed more possible, but in fact were more impossible. One feels that Wycliff's later Latin writings attack much the same problems as those troubling Langland and that Wycliff comes up with a similar, simplistic critique. In all his barbed and repetitious probings, Wycliff never tells us how in terms of an actual church or in terms of an actual political realm his purified society would voluntarily reorganize itself. His powerful criticism suggests from time to time the eventual solutions of Henry VII and Henry VIII but Wycliff himself never outlines how this new church and state could evolve a workable social contract. Ultimately, it required naked, self-interested political action, even rapacious interests, to bring a structural evolution about (not to mention the personal obsessions of monarchs).

Very real but markedly small 'local' corruptions of practice Langland could appreciate and translate into appropriate satirical exposure (the weight of a loaf of bread, for example) but the vaster, less tangible reasons for corruption escape his ability to analyse. The version of the abolition of the order of the Knights Templars which he puts into the mouth of Anima illustrates the poet's penchant for moral simplification. This is not to say that Langland cannot personify and dramatize large-scale failures, but the poet does not seem to understand why his poetic versions may be incomplete. It would have taken a very different intellectual training not only to give him the historical 'methods', but the factual evidence for arriving at analytical procedures. Pound's pseudo-renaissance ideals of a political state lead him as a poet into solutions as inappropriate and grotesque for modern society as Langland's radical 'medieval' recoveries were for his foundering and soon to be lost social institutions. A great modern historian has written: 'Langland speaks to us from a forgotten world, drowned, mysterious, irrecoverable.' Perhaps as the modern world becomes inescapably more 'medievalized' by various forms of state feudalism, Langland's original world will become more recoverable. But at the date of Langland's writing his versions of his poem, what Langland wished to see reformed and revitalized was already 'drowning'—in the process of being overwhelmed by various combinations of inadequacies: wasting decentralization, poor methods of taxation, unrealistic practices of the exchequer and central financing, vast corruption of government and laws, the wholesale practice of execution by deputies and little grasp of the principles of trade and commerce. In economic and political terms the whole fabric of what Langland wished to preserve could not be made to work. Professor Mackie's analysis seems to me just:

> ... the basic theories of church, of state, of economics, of philosophy, of life generally were set in the frame of that universalism which survived amongst the ruins of the Roman empire. The world was the special creation of God and the centre of the universe. It was an ordered unity reflecting the divine harmony of the New Jerusalem where Christ presided over the holy angels. Every individual, man or institution or idea, had being as part of the great whole from which it was derived. This great whole had several aspects and so its derivatives could be, indeed must be, arranged into several categories. But throughout the whole structure harmony prevailed. Human society was in all points regulated by a divine, universal law. There was a single church ruled by the pope, in which all ecclesiastical authority originated, and though the implications of the theory were never recognized in England, a single state governed by the emperor, from which all temporal authority was derived. In philosophy there was one single truth from which proceeded all particular truths. In morality there was one single code of righteousness; legislation was the enunciation of the eternal right rather than the formulation of anything new. In the realm of economics every article had its *justum pretium*, and the customary rents and the customary wages represented the divine institution concerning these matters.

With these complete and satisfying theories, the actual facts had at no time tallied, and as the centuries passed the discrepancies became more and more apparent. They were not unnoticed by the thinkers of the times, but, as a rule, they were either ignored or explained away by a subtle philosophy. The whole genius of the age was for harmonization and reconciliation.[2]

It was Henry VII who 'reformed' English institutions not Langland or the body of non-conformists who at one time or another were associated with Langland or Wycliff or the so-called 'Lollards'. One has heard scholars in our own day lamenting the fact that the church had never read *Piers Plowman*,—and, had they done so, had they understood the drift of Langland's criticisms, the Reformation need never have taken place. This is just wishful thinking. Once the historical, philosophical and political texts recovered from classical antiquity had been read and absorbed, and the practical results observed in the range of continental experience available, the older system of social organization was destined for either gradual or rapid reconstitution. The position of a universal church was bound to undergo extensive reform with or without benefit of Langland's call to the clergy or Christian society. What then remains of positive value in the 'historical' world of the poet's events, leaving aside for a moment the poetic 'vision' which seems to adhere (sometimes distantly) to the difficult-to-explain Dowel, Dobet and Dobest? Exactly what the renaissance itself found of value: Langland's penetrating satiric portrayals. Puttenham's characterization is worth recalling:

> He that wrote the Satyr of Piers Ploughman, seemed to haue bene a malcontent of that time, and therefore bent himselfe wholly to taxe the disorders of that age, and especially the pride of the Romane clergy, of whose fall he seemeth to be a very true Prophet ...[3]

It is plain from an earlier passage where Puttenham compares Langland with Persius and Juvenal *inter alios* that *Piers Plowman* is not by him regarded as a 'Vision' (the prevailing medieval titles are ignored) but as a type of rough satire. This is, of course, a gross renaissance distortion, yet much of the distortion contains an element of truth about what is memorable in the poem.[4] It is also worth noting that the reading public's fascination with 'satire' in Langland is much older than the renaissance interest. For built into the basic visual format of the manuscript text in the excellently paragraphed and well-copied Bodley MS. Laud Misc. 581 are indications of an earlier audience's genuine points of interest—and these interests are secular

and satiric. The evidence is provided by the clearly written, formal
nota bene marginalia. If the manuscript is as old as Mr Parkes believes
(*c.* 1390) or as late as Dr Doyle's estimated dating (*c.* 1410), it is a
very early manuscript and a very good one. I think it dates from
1425 + —but that is still sufficiently early to indicate that 'medieval'
and 'renaissance' interests in the secular and satiric dimension of the
poem were not in the least distinct.

But fourteenth- and fifteenth-century religious interests as reflected
in the poem and in the manuscript titling ('De Visione ...') cannot be
ignored. In this perhaps most Christocentric of poems, the figure of
Christ in the *visio* stands out clearly as the most memorable of
Langland's dream renderings. Passus XVIII embodied the final
justification for Truth, Justice and Mercy in Langland's critique of
Christian society. If there is a coherent philosophical or theological
bridge between the figure of Christ and the possible remedies for a
fallen and disunified society, it remains difficult, perhaps impossible,
to extract from the evidence of Langland's verses. Exactly how, as an
object of devotion or as an example for active imitation in the conduct
of our lives, this vivid image of Christ the Redeemer is meant to
operate as a transforming agent, is never made clear in the process of
the poem. Or at least I can find no sustained or convincing connecting arguments. Perhaps Langland intended the *Imago Christi* to exist
in our imaginations as if it were a Platonic Form: 'recognition' alone
would be sufficient to bring about reformation or 'correction'. If so,
then the poem remains disconnected and lacking in unity, for
'recognition' alone is not enough to unify the separate parts and
dimensions of the poem. As Professor Lawlor wisely observed long
ago, 'ideas' are insufficient. The poem must possess a demonstrable
aesthetic, imaginative unity[5]—a coherence which is memorably present in the poem itself, the tangible evidence of the poet having put it
there in the first place.

I must agree with Rosemary Woolf[6] and Dr Mills[7], that there are
cogent reasons for the lack of imaginative unity—hence the shape of
this present study. I have selected what I consider some of the striking
merits of Langland's art and some of the poet's arguable failures in
verse construction. Here and there the reader will detect an attempt
to suggest possible ways in which Langland might have attempted to
construct a sustained and unified narrative structure. But I am not
convinced by the evidence that he ever meant to bring such
'possibilities' to any form of artistic realization. The poem, for me,
remains 'a sequence of aspiration and failure'.

CHAPTER TWO

The Text and Its Evolution

They were a short flight (a dozen or so steps in all) but in that space
the baroque architect had found ways of expressing a freakish and
whimsical turn of mind, alternating high and low steps, twisting
motifs together in the most unexpected of ways, creating
superfluous little landings with niches and benches so as to produce in this small space a variety of possible joinings and separa-
tions, of brusque rejections and affectionate reconciliations, which
imparted to the staircase the atmosphere of a lovers' tiff.

> Giuseppe di Lampedusa, *Two Stories and a Memory,* Places
> of my Infancy: V The Garden.

In the present state of Langland studies, any critic of the poem
must identify the version of the work which he is going to comment on
(A, B, or C text) and now in the 1980s which modern editor's 'version' or 'reconstruction' of either of the 'A-, B-, or C- Texts' he
believes best represents what Langland may have originally written.
The choice is much wider, the differences much deeper, than they
once were. The reader of this study may be relieved, perhaps, if I
decline to accept any of the modern printed texts. The text I will offer
to comment upon will be based on a consistent B-Text of the poem in
the version represented by Bodley MS. Laud Misc. 581. My text will
look more like Bennett (Prol.-VII, Oxford, 1972) and Skeat (VIII-
XX) and not in the least like Kane and Donaldson (London, 1975) or
Schmidt (Everyman, 1978).

Now, as to the identifiable medieval versions (A, B, C): in spite of
the cleverly argued case of Professor Howard Meroney,[1] it would
seem that the generally accepted view of the stages of revison must be
acceded to. That is, the A-Text represents the earliest 'draft' of the
poem, or rather first complete version of the poem intended for
'publication'. On balance, I would accept that the relatively rare
Passus XII entire is genuine and embodies Langland's decision to use

a variation of a concluding topos (the end of an author's writing life) which had been, or was to be used, by Gower and Chaucer to successfully conclude poems. I would accept the integrity of Passus XII (A-Text) right down to the lines composed by John But[2] (Skeat, A-Text, line 104). I do not understand editors pausing to accept the genuineness of lines 99-103 and their inclination to assign these lines to But. I would agree with Professor Kane's argument (p. 40ff.) that the evidence indicates that the A-Text of the poem underwent stages of incrementation from Passus VII onwards. These indications of authorial prolongation must signify major stages of the poem's compositional development, whatever the detailed line or word readings concerned in MSS. classification. 'Incrementing' indicates clearly earliness of composing, uncertainty of intention, a first group relationship. The B-Text represents Langland's next stage of large revision, a completely new final form of the poem, beginning with the addition of all the innovative, inward, psychological questing or self-education from VIII to XV, making Passus V into a structural anticipating of XVIII. The laconic, finality of concluding rhythm of A-Text Passus XII is replaced by a return to the contemporary satiric uncertainty of the Prologue, ending in the powerful description of the army of Antichrist (borrowed from Huon de Meri, an author used elsewhere by Langland). The poem concludes with the conventional *visio* waking-topos; here, the repeated and unanswered cries of Conscience for assistance wake the poet. After all, the poem is only a thinly disguised form of self-dialogue. The C-Text represents the last stage of the evolution of a published text, augmented and revised at a later stage, perhaps as late as *c.* 1387.[3] Some of the augmentations seem to belong to Langland, but the revisions, most often *elucidationes* of the argument of the B-Text, cannot be laid at Langland's door but must be attributed to an unidentified 'editor'. These matters will be seen in a clearer perspective when we have Professor G. H. Russell's London University Press edition of the C-Text. For the medieval reader there remained a large number of copies (at least seven) of the poem made up of bastard or hybrid texts of A, B, or C origins. The habits of late medieval scriptoria confirm a state of textual conflation and contamination in the fifteenth century carried on with a total lack of recognition of the status of any of the major authorial revisions. It should be argued that the ignorance of the scriptoria concerning 'authenticity' went back earlier than the fifteenth century. It could (and should) be imagined that authorial control over the multiplication of copy never was exerted, or indeed existed—hence, the widespread evidence of 'corruption', 'contamination', and the huge degree of scribal participation reaching out well beyond the seven hybrid MSS. We have now reached a stage in textual criticism where it can be stated that there never was an uncontaminated archetype. What is surprising is that modern editors (Professor Bennett excepted) have never tried to account for this astonishing state of things, unless we are invited to subscribe to the catastrophic state theory of the origins of Langland's textual universe.

The chaotic or incoate state of the manuscripts which lies behind the establishing of the B-Text surfaced fully following the publication by the London University Press in 1975 of the Kane and Donaldson edition of the complete B-Text. In essence, the editorial method evolved by the London editors requires a radically incoate state: for their text represents a reconstruction of a copy which does not survive or, perhaps more accurately, never existed. In this editorial method 'mistakes', 'corruptions' or 'substitution' gradually become more important for scrutiny than 'true' or 'sound' readings. The London Text has been variously reviewed and the majority of reviewers I have read do not accept the London method as convincing *in toto*. Allowing for minor disagreements between reviewers, is the Kane and Donaldson method acceptable to scholarly consent? With the exception of Mr Schmidt (the Everyman editor), I suspect the method is not acceptable. One review goes right to the heart of the matter, that of Professor D. C. Fowler.[4] If we agree with his basic criticisms, then the London Text must be rejected as just another scribal version of the B-Text, a monstrous anachronism. But the reviewers and critics of the London version seem not to have asked themselves the question 'how did all this come about?'—if we accept that Kane and Donaldson's general description of the contaminated state of the manuscripts is correct. The editors and their reviewers seem to take it for granted that the editorial problems created by the contaminated state of the manuscripts of the B-Text should automatically be submitted to the solutions or types of solution applicable to some of Langland's literary contemporaries, say Chaucer or Gower. But why (ease of procedure apart) should we imagine that the same context of scribal programme existed for Langland as it did for, say, Chaucer? The fact that they (at one time or another) probably lived within walking distance of each other guarantees nothing concerning their compositional habits or their access to amanuenses. Chaucer was a gentleman of considerable means and no doubt maintained a fairly large household staff. When the young Chaucer lies awake at night he does not reach for a book on the shelf at his 'beddes hede'. He rings for a servant who fetches the book from the library or study located elsewhere in the house.[5] From the poetic evidence, he retained the services of a professional scribe who stands a good chance of being a permanent member of the Chaucer household—like an agent or private secretary of today. Chaucer's access to, and use of a professional secretary ensured a stable, regular basis for copying, and, above all, correcting. Doubtless, Chaucer kept and maintained his own original collections, both of his own work and others (including contemporaries). If the Countess of Suffolk's family library had been kept intact in the centuries following her death (and the reversion of the lordship of the manor of Ewelme to the crown), I have little doubt we, barring theft and neglect, would possess much of the Chaucer manuscript material passed on to his son Thomas and thence to Alice. Chaucer's and Thomas Chaucer's circumstances seem to have been very much like those of any comfortably-off member of the landed gentry of any historical period.

But what of Langland's mode of existence? If it remotely resembled the 'fictional' biographical glimpses we are given in the poem (especially in the C-Text), Langland's authorial life must have been very different. No safe, assured large income. No large household staff, or none at all. Certainly, no amanuensis and hence no stable, settled pattern of copying or programme of 'publication'—which includes correction and recopying. Langland's life must have been relatively unstable and unsettled and consequently his compositional methods and access to scribes must reflect his poverty and his improvised way of supporting himself and his family. This is a more reasonable assumption than the unexamined supposition that we can treat his 'text' as having emerged from the same set of conditions which produced the texts of Chaucer or Gower. Of course, all this is an assumption and cannot be 'proved', yet Langland the man must be presupposed if we are to have Langland the poet and finally his poem. If we could go back to a sentence of Professor Kane's (on the A-Text): 'The major conflation in these manuscripts is, I believe, ... a record of the availability of copies at various times and places' (p. 43). Now this seems to me undeniable and to acknowledge the real state of affairs, only I would argue on a much more radical scale. What if 'availability' was being seriously affected by Langland's unsettled and impecunious mode of life, especially that part of his life concerned with access to, and use of scribal assistance? What if this situation existed not only after the production of an A-Text, B-Text or C-Text but co-existed during all the time at which Langland was struggling to produce his poem—disturbance being exacerbated not only by the author's modest revisions but by the major revision known now as the B-Text, with its ambitious range of quest, increased length and implied complexity of structure. The more settled state of the A-Text is not just the result of shortness, but in the B-Text of the increased searching range of social and philosophical analysis creating consequent pressures on the poet and his scribal assistance, such as it was.

Let us imagine, then, an authorial situation where there is no regular access to scribal activity, no patronal dimension and consequently no need to produce or engage in the process of producing 'presentation copy', and little occasion for the author to correct working copy once it had been produced by a scribe or a collection of scribes. It is perfectly easy to visualize an authorial mode of composing which involved the poet in writing a more or less continuous fascicule evolution of the text, passus by passus or by groups of passus. Langland, if he had no single, regular amanuensis would have had to have put the fascicules out to be copied at a commercial scriptorium or perhaps set of scriptoria where the scribes would be contracted for and paid piecemeal. There would be no consistency or regularity of production, with little or no opportunity for a continuity of authorial over-seeing or correction. Granted that this account might describe the method of composition and copying which Langland was obliged to engage in, then the detectable age of any manuscript (no matter how early) would prove of little value to the textual scholar, for within whatever space of time occupied by multiplication by scriptoria or stationers, the whole textual issue would have become muddled. 'Coincident variation' would be but a small tip of the iceberg. The scribal copies retained by the author would have lacked adequate correcting and subsequent recopying. In all the copies manifested (including the authorial copy) scribal participation would have remained high because of the lack of supervision. Professor Kane even imagines an 'augmenter'. It is not so much a question of whether or not the poet was sufficiently interested in correcting copy but that circumstances prevented the exercise of authorial interest. Apart from the author's collection of passus, copy arrived at piecemeal and without benefit of consistent supervision, there would exist no 'archetype' available for further multiplication in the ordinary way in which we use the term. The genesis of a 'corrected version' had never been a part of the process of 'publication' in the normal course of medieval book production. Random and perhaps serial multiplication and sale by scriptoria and stationers fuelled by the poem's topicality and intense popular interest in the poet's social criticism became the unsupervised result of the authorial and scribal situation I am trying to reconstruct. It is exactly what the extant manuscripts seem to confirm. After exhaustive collation by the London editors, the attempt at producing 'recensions', the effort to classify into 'substantive groups', it would seem as if no significant order can be extracted from the manuscript evidence. So another, intensely detailed, editorial procedure (in no way new or original, but never so exhaustively exploited) is elaborated to arrive at a state of purity or integrity which we cannot prove had ever come into existence. In my view, purification of the text is not only impossible but perhaps was never seriously considered by the author as a literary *desideratum*.

This impossibility of 'purifying' is especially applicable to the B-Text manuscripts. For here the London editors admit that what they call the 'archetype' was itself defective or contaminated. What textual point is there in performing this excruciatingly detailed activity if what we are trying to create never existed in the first place? It is vain to argue that it once existed but did not survive, for all the extant manuscript copies came into being at a very serious remove from the putative 'archetype', two removes, actually—date and existence. The London editors, recognizing the extent of the state of corruptness in all the manuscripts, make a series of editorial decisions. Quite rightly they reject the old 'recension' by stemma or some type of formal classification (p. 55). By p. 113 they are summarizing the difficulty, then the impossibility, of constructing 'genetic listings'. Thereafter the editors increasingly come to be obsessed with a detailed study and classification of the erroneous, or rather the putatively erroneous—that is, how hypothetical 'variants' or possible scribal substitutions were generated. This detailed reconstruction of what might arguably lie behind erroneous readings (once these have been identified and accounted for) comes to dominate editorial thinking on the grounds that the editor can reconstruct what was once written by Langland before the 'error' or 'substitution' had been made by a scribe or scribes. Of course, the assumption is that the original or purified reading may be attributable to Langland. If the manuscript evidence is as contaminated or as dominated by scribal participation as I think it was, then the restored readings may turn out to be just another set of scribal substitutions or stage of scribal participation. It is not a very certain method. Imagine trying to reconstruct Milton's *Paradise Lost* from a batch of written manuscripts dating from the eighteenth century already altered by extensive emendation by not just Bentley but several of his pupils. Could we reconstruct the Miltonic original, not even knowing which lines or words were suspect in the first place? Homer's ghost in Lucian's *Veræ Historiæ* when asked if he had composed the lines and words published in square brackets craftily replied: 'certainly'.

Gradually and with great meticulousness the London editors 'cleanse' the text of the B-Text by accounting for every case of putative scribal substitution even on the minutest scale. In the process 'originality' or 'authenticity' become a 'statistical probability'—the phrase is used. Having openly rejected the old and discredited democratic mathematical count of the Root and Manly and Rickert type, the method is reintroduced as a form of normative reconstruction: when all unexplained and unaccountable scribal substitutions have been eliminated from the list of variants and which therefore cannot be assigned to normative groups. This is, of course, a dangerous use of a classifying short-cut. There is a crucial case in B-Text, Passus II, 205 which illustrates the point I am trying to make. Lines 205-207 read in nearly all manuscripts:

> Drede atte dore stode and þe dome herde,
> And how þe kynge comaunded constables and seriantʒ
> Falsenesse and his felawschip to fettren an to bynden.

Professor Bennett rightly observes in his notes (p. 132):

> *dome* (cf. A *doom*) may seem inappropriate, as no sentence has been pronounced; several MSS, of all three versions *dyne* ('noise') or variants: R. W. Chambers, *MLR* 31 (1926), 31-4 and Kane [1960 edn. of A-text], p. 437. The reference in *dyne* might be one to the custom of crying the name(s) of the parties summoned at the door of the royal council chamber (Baldwin, *The King's Council*, p. 294).

This seems to me an interesting case, for you could argue that the 'conscience' implied in the 'fear' here is the guilty conscience of

Meed's rabble and that the malefactors' Fear is anticipating the king's as yet undelivered judgment. Or you could argue that *dome* should be weakened so as to mean 'order' (*MED dom* 3 (a)) or 'decision' (*MED dom* 4 (a)). But however you gloss the passage, 'sentence' or 'judgment' will not do, at least not without argument. The fused poetic and realistic texture of the passage is increased if the final authorial reading was *dyne*, for one function of the royal serjeants-at-arms was to walk the corridors outside the king's chambers calling out the names of the accused. It would not have to be a guilty Fear who heard this. But in the London apparatus to the B-Text, the variant *dyne*, *dyune* is not listed; either it is a mechanical error of no consequence or it is too small statistically for classification into a normative group and hence escapes recording. No one reading Kane and Donaldson or Schmidt (though Schmidt notes Bennett's objection) would be aware that there might be a textual problem in these lines. Skeat himself did not record the variant for one supposes he assumed *dome* was the correct reading and probably understood the sense 'decision'—a sense he records as Langland's usage in Passus XV.

May there not, then, be a host of similar cases where on some statistical accounting, important and crucial variants have been mechanically eliminated from representation, and therefore, discussion? By the same argument a vast number of unsubstantive and meaningless 'substitutions' must have been admitted to classification if numerously repeated. But worse is to follow. The London editors' 'normalization' of types of alliterative lines *causa metri* by analogy with late OE types and the metrical practice of the A-Text is even more of a catastrophe. As Professor Bennett wisely commented in his Clarendon edition (p. viii):

> I have rarely emended on metrical or alliterative grounds alone, since it is impossible to be sure what variation the poet (as distinct from the copyists) allowed himself within an accepted alliterative pattern.

The rhythmical movement of the A-Text has always struck me as slower and more regular than the wonderful velocity and plasticity of movement of the B-Text, a special new characteristic which is sustained throughout all the poet's new version. To make the B-Text sound like the A-Text is peculiarly insensitive. All this editorial interference makes a complete mullock of the text. Kane and Donaldson have turned themselves into another set of scribes. We now have a strange and expensive anachronism: a printed copy of MS. KD (xx *sæc.* ³/₄).

What should, then, the modern editor do about arriving at a reasonably authentic text, given the limited definition of 'authentic' arising out of the special nature of the Langland authorial situation? Frankly, I think the editor will be obliged to go back to where Professor Skeat left off. Armed with the increased evidence of recent collation, he should review the possibility of classification roughly into groups which may reflect substantive authorial decisions. Then, it remains for the editor to select the least corrupted manuscript of that group as a base-text and edit it in the usual way, eschewing all attempts at 'normalization' and constant minute emendation. In other words, exactly what Professor Bennett did in editing the B-Text Prol.-VII for the Clarendon Press.[6] If the ghost of Langland were contacted (in the Lucianian spirit) and asked which one of the extant manuscripts of the B-Text most accurately represented what he had written, he might well reply (after the manner of Homer's ghost), 'I honestly don't know'. Unless Langland retained a clean and systematically corrected (as well as revised) copy of the B-Text, he himself could not have 'restored' an authentic version, for the poet may have revised so much and so intermittently in addition to never having been in a position to carry out extensive correction, that his memory of the 'finality' of the text would have been serious impaired. This state of impaired memory is often encountered when dealing with living poets. Langland probably could not have identified scribal substitution in any more than a very few cases of minutiæ. He could be imagined as testifying on the authenticity of larger units—say, Passus XII of the A-Text. But the mass of detailed variants might defeat his ability to recognize them. He might even be imagined as preferring some scribal 'inventions' as superior to his own—if he could have identified them. The modern text of Langland, relatively free of obvious 'errors' can only be achieved along broad outlines; and all the recent resources of improved palæographical analysis and description[7] allied to all the sophisticated explanations of modern textual procedure will take us no further in any realistic direction. Older methods will probably achieve as much as is possible, certainly as much as is desirable, given the original authorial and scribal context of manuscript composition and production.

A further question arises if we consider the continuous, fascicular, piecemeal, commerical copying situation as a probable cause of the state of Langland manuscripts in all three versions, with varying degrees of emphasis. This question touches on the actual literary shape of the poem itself. Can the piecemeal, highly random, authorially unsupervised evolution of the text be taken to explain the nature of the literary shape of the poem? Can the very frequent signs of repetitiousness, digressiveness and lack of narrative coherence have derived from the problems associated with textual evolution? It would be wrong, I think, to put too much blame on the mechanics of this process. The formal problem in *Piers Plowman* has its roots more deeply sunk in the question of the kind of formal models Langland may have had in mind, or more significantly, did not have in mind. Langland shows a very narrow range of strictly literary reading, if we compare him with his great contemporaries. Yet if we compare the more politically oriented *visio* of Gower's *Vox Clamantis*, we find a more orderly or logical disposition into units of books, but the smaller *partes* or *capita* within the *libri* of the *Vox* are often little better organized than *Piers Plowman* and nearly always lack Langland's poetic vitality, however 'polished' the elegaic distichs. The obvious model which may be imagined to lie behind both *visiones* may be the accumulative and loosely organized apparent shape of the socially critical 'satire', especially that form descending from Juvenal's *Satires* via the post-twelfth-century types of *Satura Communis*. The wholly barbarous *De Contemptu Mundi* inherits all Juvenal's superficial attributes: the remorseless tone of *indignatio*, the pithiness of exemplary *emphasis*, the marshalling of contrasting episodes and larger antithetical narrative rhythms and movements, the habit of swooping in on details—the sudden movings from larger scenes into smaller or even minute perspectives. But the medieval Latin poem shows not the slightest appreciation of the range of unifying techniques which gives Juvenal's work an underlying strength of coherent structure.[8] Poetic social commentary and criticism which descends from this branch of Roman formal satire would have encouraged medieval authors to compose loosely organized, accumulative structures. Both Juvenal and Persius are dangerous authors to imitate. The structural refinements and subtleties of Horace seem to have been beyond most medieval authors with the notable exception of Geoffrey Chaucer.[9] Langland's artistic culture is not that of the well-read, urbane literary gentleman. His art belongs to the engrafting, scissors-and-paste, amalgamating side of the creative process of medieval imaginative activity.

CHAPTER THREE

Langland's Poetry: Form and Style

In principles and essential characteristics it contrasts most violent-
ly with classical architecture, and although many of the general
forms and features were constantly undergoing important alterations, the principles remained unchanged till the final extinction of
the style: it is thus defined by Mr. Whewill: 'It is characterized by
the pointed arch; by pillars which are extended so as to lose all
trace of classical proportions; by shafts which are placed side by
side, often with different thicknesses, and are variously clustered
and combined. Its mouldings, cornices and capitals, have not the
classical shapes and members; square edges, rectangular surfaces,
pilasters and entablatures disappear; the elements of building
become slender, detached, repeated and multiplied; they assume
forms implying flexure and ramification.'

    J. H. Parker, *A Glossary of Terms used in Grecian, Roman,
    Italian and Gothic Architecture,* 5th edn., 3 vols. (Oxford,
    1850), vol. i., p. 338.

'detached, repeated and multiplied ... forms implying flexure and
ramification.' The words are early Victorian and belong to the renew-
ing of modern interest in a detailed study of the architecture of the
Middle Ages and attempts to find a descriptive language for what was
called 'Gothic'.[1] Although William Whewell may have been
anticipated by Stonehouse by a little (1839) in the use of 'flexure' as
applied to architecture, 'ramification' is here applied for the first time
in English to the general principles of medieval architectural invention. The terminology seems apt for describing the tendencies of
Langland's poetic architectonics, although it may seem perverse to
turn back to the 1840s to find suitable expressions when more recent
studies have been busy to formulate theories and vocabulary which
will account for the formal tendencies of Langland's poem. By
eschewing modern accounts we escape from the prevailing drift of

nearly all such criticism: a desire to evolve a descriptive and analytic vocabulary which will demonstrate the existence of a successful unity in the poem. By and large, Langland's twentieth-century academic critics have tried (not with conspicuous success) to 'save appearances'. Most of these studies begin zealously enough, then gradually lose confidence. Some types of inquiry acknowledge their loss of faith, for example, Professor M. W. Bloomfield's *Piers Plowman as a Fourteenth-Century Apocalypse*, New Jersey, (1962) openly reflects on the author's inability to trace convincingly the origin of the scheme of Dowel, Dobet and Dobest. Other scholars are less candid and less original. The most useful studies seem to me to amount to honest, patient exegeses of the 'argument' of the poem and the concepts which may lie behind Langland's criticisms of his society and his 'solutions'. Professor R. W. Frank's *Piers Plowman and the Scheme of Salvation*, New Haven, (1957) is one of the best of these elucidations. But whatever clarification his study affords, I can find nowhere in it a sustained critical analysis of literary and formal problems presented by Langland's poem. Most modern salvationists of Langland's literary unity may be classified as 'coat-tailers' or 'bandwaggoners': they assert that a convincing theory of formal unity has already been evolved by a collection of other criticis (named and summarized) and then modestly add a few more refinements (or crudifications) of their own. The main burden of proof invariably lies in some other account or tradition of accounts. It is critical language as gesture. The commonest form of proof is argument by reference to thematic structures or 'repetitions' or 'recapitulations'[2], often in combination ('a pattern of repeated symbols and themes'), often attended by a variety of other aducements, numerological, theological, scholastic-philosophical, moral and experiential. How perceptive Whewell was in 1842. You will notice the crucial present participle in his description of 'the Gothic': 'forms *implying* flexure and ramification'. There is a strong element of illusion and implication in the school he is attempting to describe—a school unlike the rectilinear clarity of classical forms: 'square edges ... surfaces'. The same or similar implications, implications of an underlying wholeness, exist, too, in Langland's poem; but that 'wholeness' is not actually present in the formal structure. It is implied as existing in various relationships between separate members of a Christian society, or as existing between the individual moral consciousness and the 'debt' it owes to the powers or Power which brought it into existence and shaped its 'faculties' for cognition. It is sometimes identified with 'Kynde Witte', as the relation-ship or social implication is sometimes identified with the functions of Dowel, Dobet and Dobest. This is one reason for the search for coherent unity in the poem by elucidations of the poem's ideas—Langland was already gesturing in that direction. It helps to account for the social direction of the search for plausible unity, for finding coherence in the application of ideas to the shape and function of medieval secular or religious society. This wholeness had always been implied by the political evangelists or propagandists for that feudality which was 'continually undergoing important alteration'. Consider these modern words of Jacquetta Hawkes in trying to distinguish between one activity of the Renaissance (exploitation of natural resources) and the Middle Ages[3]:

> Behind this innovation [mining and clearance of forests], this new relationship that allowed large numbers of men to plunder the land and no longer to seek its fertility, a change in the direction of human consciousness was gathering momentum. The Christianity of the Middle Ages had been a means for reuniting consciousness with its surroundings. It had fostered an intuitive life where mind still drew much of its deepest levels and saw the whole material as the symbols of a reality of which it was a part.

These words, written in the 1950s could have been penned by Welby Pugin and added to his *Contrasts* published in 1836, two years after his conversion to the Roman church. Had governments or powerful magnates of the medieval period been able to exploit natural resources on a grand scale no doubt they would have. What they could, and did, exploit was human life itself, incorporating human nature into a technological definition of itself, into a network of bind-ing 'mechanical servitudes' of one kind or another. Obligatory func-tion is the lifeblood of feudalism. One must doubt whether this seeing of 'the whole material world as the symbol of a reality of which it was a part' constitutes an absolute truth. In the continuous process of historical evolution it amounts to a 'version' of a conceptualized reali-ty, another model world.[4] But the model, no matter how 'intuitive' of wholeness or systematically logical in the philosophical proofs of the 'oneness of existence' cannot provide an arguable basis for formal unity of design in a work of art. That 'unity' exists as the creation of the artist or poet, it cannot be supplied by theologians, philosophers or social historians or churches. It is to be detected in the aesthetic product, not even in the putative 'mind' of the producer. Years ago, the late Nevill Coghill once confided: 'if Langland did do his thinking in allegory, perhaps Lewis was right.' I took it he was referring to Lewis's distinction between allegory as a mode of expression not thought. Often it seems as if Langland is thinking when he should have been writing and writing when he should have been thinking. After all, in the great stretch of the poem which is most an inward search, where the landscape and characters should be most coloured by the mind of the poet (Passus VIII-XV) we find the poem weakest in sustained narrative expression as well as self-expressiveness, a depressing sequence of false turnings, cul-de-sacs, and miles of boot-sucking mud. At the same time, it yields us brilliant set-pieces of sustained satiric portraiture, of a vivid naturalness unrivalled by the confessing sins of Passus V: the shrewish, husband-dazing hot-gospeller of Education, Dame Study; the greedy and devious 'Doctor'; that mundane and mendacious Mr Jingle, Haukin. It often seems as if the broken-winded narrative has somehow been obscurely designed to throw up these false prophets of elucidation. Until, that is, we reach Passus XVIII to find that the baffling and seemingly downward spiral of the narrative quest has been designed for the great Christian moment of paradoxical action: the Passion of Christ and the Atonement—'sunk low, but mounted high'. But the formal process, the narrative control, has plainly been undermined by the ultimate religious and moral implication. Reflection and expression are too confused, too close together, both in the narrator's experience and our experience. Langland has created no space, no sense of definiteness, no expansive connectedness which the horizontal, forward movement of sequential narrative requires. Langland's conviction or belief is never in doubt, the majestic creation of Passus XVIII and the urgent support of *caritas* in Passus XVII will convince the most sceptical of readers. The problem lies in the formal expression of this conviction:

It is not an easy poem to understand or to describe briefly, for Langland was careless of poetic art, and careful only to put into the most forceful of words the many ideas that a deep knowledge of the England of his day had impressed upon him. He is satirist, critic, reformer, and many other things, but all are directed to the creating of a new state of affairs in the realm so that Righteousness and Truth shall prevail ... A deeply felt conviction underlies the poet's message and gives power to the wealth of argument, illustration, anecdote, allegory and realism by which it is conveyed. Langland uses every means in his power, *not as a result of conscious art*, but as a part of his overwhelming anxiety to convince his countrymen of what must be done if England is to be a Christian country.[5]

Although I do not agree that Langland was burning to create 'a new state of affairs' (Langland was an arch-conservationist), this old-fashioned view seems to me nearer the truth than more recent attempts to 'save appearances', to justify by conjuring up spurious unity where there is only a conspicuous lack of 'conscious art'. How conscious was Langland of his own compositional activity? The evidence for this must be sought in the poem—and the self-conscious passages are few and not especially revealing. Professor Bennett in a discussion of Chaucer's 'agnostic reservation' which accompanies comments on the nature of dreams in the *Parliament* (106) observed: 'Langland likewise quotes Cato's *ne somnia cures*, and we do not think of Langland as an *esprit fort.* '[6] From the poet's passing comments we glimpse little that is not 'orthodox' and strongly coloured by a certain lack of sympathy for the art of poetry.

There are two balancing passages which open the poem (Prologue 33-9) and close the *visio* in the epilogic section (Passus VII. 143-172). The deliberate placing of these comments on poetic composition strengthens and supports the view that the *visio* unit (Prologue-Passus VII) has been shaped into a separate pattern in the B-Text.[7] The phrase in Passus VIII. 2: 'Al a somer sesoun' is designed to recall the opening words of the Prologue: 'In a somer sesoun', just as the concluding lines of Passus VII embody a traditional rhythm of a closing prayer. In the *exordium* the flavour of the phraseology no doubt recalls other Middle English poems using variations of the wording. Professor Bennett quotes *Somer Sunday* and the *Parlement of the Thre Ages*, but there are others, *In a semely someres tyde* (*Index* 1456, dated from the fifteenth century) and *In a noon tide of a somers day* (*Index* 1454,) which may reflect the same, *exordium*, rhetorical positioning. Lines 33-39 of the Prologue read:

And somme murthes to make as mynstralles conneth,
And geten gold with here glee giltles, I leue.
Ac iapers and iangelers, Iudas chylderen,

Feynen hem fantasies and foles hem maketh,
And han here witte at wille to worche, ȝif þei sholde;

Lines 33-34 seem to absolve 'entertainments' as long as they are
recreative and assigned to the world of harmless minstrelsy. We can
gather from the *Hous of Fame* where Chaucer ranked this level of activity. The personalizing and qualifying 'I leue' is a little suspicious.
Professor Bennett sees the poet 'balancing between various ways of
life'. But who exactly does Langland mean by 'iangelers'? Itinerant
jongleurs? Certainly, the two nouns are paired in Passus X.31. Here
the context suggests nothing as general as 'jesters' but should perhaps
refer to some more specific activity professed or practised as a skill.
Perhaps 'poets' might be so described? By the time of the evolution of
the C-Text the two distinct and possibly 'balanced' groups have
disappeared and 'murthes' itself is condemned. Even the harmless
recreative activity has been censured (C-Text, 35-40). The condensed
reference in line 39 to Ephesians 5.4. should alert us to the fact that
Langland's 'I nel nought preve it here' is a casual rendering of Paul's
'nec nominatur in vobis'—it is not so much that Langland is afraid of
slandering anyone, as he is being ostentatiously oblique and guarded.
This undermines one's confidence in the plain meaning of the words.
Instead, it calls attention to the range of possibilities of application.
When we come to the Latin leonine verses of lines 132-138 (not by
Langland, cf. Lambeth MS. 61, fol. 147b. and Bennett's note, p. 99),
the poet again becomes extremely oblique. The reciter of these crude
but seemingly popular lines is introduced into the action as if he were
a pageant angel (in the midst if the 'realism' there is something iden-
tifiably unreal here) and an answer is returned by a mysterious and
unidentified 'goliardeys'. Then we hear a verse riposte by the Commons who utter a dangerous political maxim in the same Latin
measure. Langland's implied warning: 'Contrue hoso wolde' might
almost be rendered: 'translate it, whoever dares'. Poetry seems to be
a dangerous activity in more ways than one—more than a little
'shady'. Three further references to verse-making within the first *visio*
section do little to restore one's confidence. We meet with 'myrthe
and mynstralcye' again at the start of Passus III where this burst of
jollity is introduced 'Mede to plese'. Not a happy conjunction. Worse
is to follow: 'Mynstrelles' in line 132 are declared by Conscience to be
in Meed's hire (and cf. line 219). In Pasus IV. 16, Reason exempts
the school-boy *Disticha Catonis* (one of Langland's favourite texts)

from censure by commending his honesty and pairing him with the popular Tommy True-Tongue. This is not a vote for sophisticated or cultivated writing.

If we take the epilogue passage (VII. 143-172 ff.) which reflects on the truthfulness of 'dreams' as reflecting on his own poetic compositions in the form of dreams, we should note, again, the tone of guarded scepticism:

> Ac I haue no sauoure in songewarie, for I se it ofte faille.
> Catoun and canonistres conseilleth vs to leue
> To sette sadnesse in songewarie, for *sompnia ne cures.*
>   Ac for þe boke bible bereth witnesse
> How Danyel deuyned þe dremes of a kynge
> Þat was Nabugodonosor nemped of clerkis.
>
> (VII. 148-153)

Honest 'Cato' is cited against *somnia* and the trouble of interpreting them. Immediately Biblical 'dreams' are opposed as undoubted expressions of truth. All of this reminds one of Chaucer's discussion in the *praefatio* of the *House of Fame*. But Chaucer used this argumentative topos exactly as Guillaume de Lorris had in the *Roman* (lines 1-20), as a beginning-motif, whereas Langland introduces it almost as if it were a closing apology—or partial apology—for the 'epilogue' seems to falter and rambles on extending the discussion to include the validity of types of pardons. Line 167 ('And al þis maketh me on þis meteles to þynke') indicates that Langland means to associate his poem, his dream, with an act of significant and truthful composition (worthy of being interpreted); but the verses which follow drift away into 30 odd lines of recapitulation and more observations on the act of pardoning. One feels that the poet has taken his eye off the object. The lines are unpointed, qualifying, and sound conversationally digressive, even though the identification of Dowel with Christ's commands (line 199 looks back to line 190) conveys a sense of rhythmical firmness at the very end of the concluding prayer.

What does Langland vouchsafe us about 'conscious art' in the long, psychological unfolding of the *vitæ* from Passus VIII to Passus XV? Very little that is positively enlightening, I fear. Passus VIII contains a glancing reference to bird-song:

> Blisse of þo briddes brouȝte me aslepe
> And vnder a lynde vppon a launde lened I a stounde,

To lyche þe layes þo louely foules made.
Murthe of her mouthes made me þere to slepe;

(VIII. 64-67) [fol. 34a]

The bird-song, imagined as 'poetry' is the sleep-inducing agent which corresponds with the sound of the flowing brook ('it sweyved so merye') of Prologue 9-10 and serves to introduce us to his 'Thought'. But all the elements of this natural *descriptio* are conventional and applied in a very general spirit. The application of *layes* to birds is a widespread and popular commonplace. So, too, the alliterating choice of a tree, 'a lynde vpon a launde'. One feels the mechanical operation of the sounds, the hypnotic sonority, invoked as a bridge between waking and sleeping is more important to Langland's art than a particular sensitivity of the poet to any kind of 'music of nature'. An addition to the C-Text might make us pause, though: 'and here loueliche notes' (l. 65).

We hear no more about verse-making until we are ushered into the hypercritical and complaining presence of Dame Study. Of 'iogeloures and iangelers of gestes' she says:

Þei conne namore mynstralcye ne musyke men to glade,
Than Munde the mylnere of *multa fecit deus*.

(X. 43-44) [fol. 38a]

We should expect this observation from her. The puzzling reference to the words of Psalm 39.6 perhaps contains a punning criticism of the Miller's dishonesty in taking his tax or toll in an amount of grain. There is much on this subject in the *Reeve's Tale*. The medieval Latin word for the Miller's toll was *multura* (cf. MED, *Multur* n.), and although a development of medieval Latin *molitura*, we can easily imagine the Miller's praise on taking his unjust due reading 'multura fecit Deus'. Lines 48-50 take us back to Langland's observations in Prologue 33-39:

Ac murthe and mynstralcye amonges men is nouthe
Leccherye, losen erye and loseles tales;
Glotenye and grete othes, þis murthe thei louieth.

The C-Text suppresses the Dame's concern with a decline in minstrelsy. Later in her tirade we meet (in a very odd and jumbled account of the *Artes* and the *auctores curriculi*) a reference to 'Plato the poete' (171)—and, more grievous still, as an 'introductory' text! The agent noun 'poet' only means an 'inspired writer' (in general use, cf. medieval Latin *poeta, vates*), compare B-Text X.340 and Alan of Lille, *Anticlaudianus* I. 133-134. In Passus XI (36) the 'poete Plato' is attributed with a Christian proverb. None of this tells us much about Langland's attitude to the art poetical, and Langland's last mention of minstrelsy in Passus XIII (224) connects the unreliable and corrupt Haukin with the activity. Although suppressed in the C-Text version perhaps by 'editing', 'Ymaginatyf' (Langland's own *vis imaginativa*[8]) accuses his 'master' (B-Text, XII.16) 'And þow medlest þe with makynges ...'. The tone is hostile and Langland lamely acknowledges the accusation that he is wasting his time in composing poetry. The poet's defence (hardly adequate) amounts to:

> I seigh wel he sayde me soth, and somewhat me to excuse,
> Seide, 'Catoun conforted his sone that, clerke þough he were,
> To solacen hym sum tyme as I do whan I make;
> *Interpone tuis interdum gaudia curis etc.*

[fol. 49b]

No one could build a 'Defence of Poetry' on *Disticha Catonis* III.7.

One cannot supply Langland's form and style from the author's own consciousness of his art. On his own admission he thinks of himself as a 'maker', and his productions as 'makinges' (the etymology of *poesis* and *poeta* was well-known to the Middle Ages). What sort of 'making' is Langland attempting? Although all the elements of Langland's 'style' already existed and were no doubt familiar to his potential audience, the blending together of these elements has the accumulative effect of creating a new type of poetic construction. In Langland's hands the *visio* genre is applied to religious purposes, social criticism and satire with a distinctive and detailed urgency of contemporary reference which we do not find in any of the *visiones* as applied to similar areas in other poems previously circulated. We find political application in the *Parlement of Thre Ages* but the alliterative pace and formal construction is nothing like Langland. For example, the dreamer dissolves from the poem as soon as the dream emerges. The narrator-figure exists on another, separate, plane (which includes a lengthy pseudo-autobiographical account). Similarly, in *Wynner and Wastour* and *Deth and Liffe*, the dreamer-observer evaporates or becomes a transparent observer. In all three poems all protagonists participate in an identifiable debate. In *Deth and Liffe* the protagonist wins outright, in *Wynner and Wastour* the personage who arbitrates (the kyng) decides. Only in the *Parlement of the Thre Ages* is the reader left in any uncertainty as to the type of debate. In all three poems what is strongest in Langland, an abiding and developing impression of the dreamer's character (almost a measurable biographical presence) is totally absent.[9] The velocity of pace, the conversational lightness, variability and quickness of transitions of Langland's alliterative lines and poetic paragraphs have little counterpart in these poems or in the *Gawain*-poet's works. Where the alliterating factor is low in many passages of *Piers Plowman*, especially in the B-Text style, the verse has the spontaneous and continuous rhythmical movement of blank verse.[10] Of course, all alliterative verse shares a basic 'phraseological' emphasis[11] owing to the residual tendencies of a common origin: the tendency of alliterative pairing to produce stave-units with marked midline caesural pause which cause us to 'hear' in half-lines and chief-letters and sub-letters that depend on primary and secondary stressing. The effect of phraseological emphasis is not primarily rhythmic (though that is its inventive origin) but grammatical since it trains the poet's ear to exploit types of syntactical shape and order which best serve the stave-unit's preservation of identity, and therefore restrict plasticity of continuous movement and variation in the placing of the rhythmical caesura within the whole line unit. Composition of Ovidian end-stopped couplets imposes a similar set of unit restrictions on a poet writing in Latin or English. But since the unit in Latin lacks rime accentuation and only requires metrical regularity (more pronounced in the pentameter half of the unit) where the native accentual tendency can freely be at variance with the metrical framework, the Latin poet can achieve grammatical plasticity and variation more easily—aided by the wonderful freedom of not being tied down to types of fixed syntactical sentence or clause order. English poets must work harder to achieve grammatical variety and extension. Sandys and Pope tended to be successful in creating suspensive and continuous poetic syntax in riming couplets. Dryden and Cleveland tended not to be so successful. Of the alliterative poets of the fourteenth century, Langland in the B-Text achieves a more pronounced plasticity and continuousness of movement than any of his contemporaries, although the *Gawain*-poet shows much the same inventive ability in passages of conversation and dialogue.

Let us take a specimen passage at random from the poem and see what effects the poet creates by alliterative composing and what

stylistic attributes can be extracted. I have opened my text at Passus I
and my eye falls on lines 43-70:

> 'Madame, mercy,' quod I, 'me liketh wel ȝowre wordes,
> Ac þe moneye of þis molde þat men so faste holdeth,
> Telle me to whom, madam, þat tresore appendeth?'
> 'Go to þe gospel,' quod she, 'þat God seide hymseluen,
> Tho þe poeple hym apposed wiþ a peny in þe temple,
> Whether þei shulde þerwith worschip þe kyng Sesar.
> And God axed of hem of whome spake þe lettre,
> And þe ymage ilyke þat þereinne stondeth
> "*Cesaris*," þei seide, "we sen hym wel vchone."
> "*Reddite Cesari*," quod God, "þat *Cesari* bifalleth.
> *Et que sunt dei, deo* or elles ȝe done ille."
> For riȝtful Reson shulde rewle ȝowe alle,
> And Kynde Witte be wardeyne, ȝowre welthe to kepe,
> And tutour of ȝoure tresore and take it ȝow at nede:
> For housbonderye and hij holden togideres.'
> Þanne I frained hir faire, for hym þat hir made:
> 'That dongeoun in þe dale þat dredful is of siȝte,
> What may it be to mene, madame, I ȝow biseche?'
> 'Þat is þe castel of care; whoso cometh þerinne
> May banne þat he borne was to body or to soule.
> Þerinne woneith a wiȝte þat Wronge is yhote,
> Fader of falshed, and founded it hymselue.
> Adam and Eue he egged to ille,
> Conseilled Caym to kullen his brother;
> Iudas he iaped with Iuwen siluer,
> And sithen on an eller honged hym after.
> He is letter of loue and lyeth hem alle;
> That trusten on his tresor bitrayeth he sonnest.'

I would notice about a dozen stylistic points. (1) In spite of the social
distance between the lady of the castle Truth and the dreamer, there
is a certain naturalness of conversational exchange. It is impossible to
tell whether this reflects ordinary English social usage, or has been
much modified by literary convention. After initial frictions, Boethius
and Philosophia achieve a certain naturalness of exchange in
dialogue. In this passage a minimum of politeness is maintained
especially on the poet-dreamer's part: 'madame' is often repeated as a
mark of respect. The lady leaves the dreamer unacknowledged by the

courtesy of any title, an open 'neutrality' or 'transparency' is employed by the lady as a mode of social indifference, and therefore superiority. Both speakers keep to the polite second person plural, but the usage is not consistent, cf. Holy Church's use of the singular pronoun in lines 35, 37, 38, 39, 40, 41, 42, 75, 76, 78, etc. (2) There is a reasonable variation in the length of the poetic period. The normal maximum length appears to be about three lines with only a slight pause at the ends of line units. The grammatical length shortens in the terse descriptions of Adam and Eve and Cain. This is deliberate emphatic, exemplary pointing. (3) The examples of *le style coupé* apart, the normal syntax is of a long, loose construction type, it is not suspensive or interlocked. Subordination is not the rule. Langland's English syntax is of a natural, modern cast. Apart from a few syntactical items (*e.g., Ac, tho, ilyke, that, sithen*), three verbs (*frainen, bannen, wonien*) and a very few inflectional verb markers, the passage could easily convert into early modern English of a not very literary flavour. (4) In tune with the syntax there is variation in alliterative emphasis. Hard consonantal stress becomes stronger and more pronounced when moral and educative points are required to be memorable (54-56) and 65-67. (5) There is also Langland's habitual recourse to Latin quotation. Here Latin phrases are employed as a realistic part of the conversational exchange between the Jewish people and Christ. There is a mixture of Latin and ME within the sentence and we must not call this *macaronic*[12]. In this passage the mixed lines derive from a common dramatic convention used in the 'Mystery Plays'. The same convention is employed by the drama in the sixteenth century. The Latin quotation also lends authority to the evidence as well as dramatic immediacy. (6) Langland's intuitive appreciation of the force of verbs is represented. There is emphatic use of arresting monosyllabic verbs in the phrase 'egged to ille' and 'iaped with silver' where the verb *iapen* incorporates at least three senses: 'tricked', 'mocked', and 'made a fool of'. (7) There is a marked predominance of *prosopopoeia* (personification) over *translatio* (metaphor). I notice four examples of probable personification: *Reson, Kynde Witte, Wrong, Care*. These are focused on moral qualities: two are 'internalized' virtues or mental functions assigned psychological activity; one is a vice (with psychological colouring) and one is a *passio* (strong emotion) also with psychological application. (8) The metaphoric activity in this passage arises chiefly out of the personifications. Here we are moving in the direction of connected similitude or miniature *allegoria*.

Reson is imagined as having a ruling function (the metaphor is implied in the verb), and Kynde Witte (innate moral conscience) functions as *wardeyne of welthe* and *tutour of tresore* in a pair of alliterating phrases. 'Warden' probably only signifies 'keeper' or 'guardian', but the chief officer of the Mint was designated 'Warden' by the 1460s. Still, the context is domestic in these lines. 'Tutor' has the usual ME sense (shared by late Latin) of 'guardian', although the educational application may be touched on here. The pronoun 'hij' in line 57 confirms the status of personification in Reson and Kynde Witte. (9) There is one basic *allegoria* in the 'Castle of Care'[13] which has a personified inhabitant Wronge (Satan) who is probably the architect, 'founded it hymselfe'. I do not think this is the abstract verb 'established' but may signify the actual physical building of the Castel (the use is well-attested in ME). This little *allegoria* probably does not derive from erudite literary usage (compare the *domus* in Chaucer's *House of Fame* which reflects a reading knowledge of Virgil, Ovid, Statius, Alan of Lille and Dante *inter alios*). Langland's model is perhaps less learned. We know that he had read Grosseteste's *Casteau d'Amour* and we meet 'Castels' of this and that in the Old French poets Raoul de Houdanc and Huon de Meri (whom he had also read). There appears to be a contemporary ME expression 'caymes castel' (= a Friary) in the Wycliffite writings. Certainly the expression can be traced to Wycliff's Latin writings; we find in the tract *De Fundatione Sectarum* (cap. vii)[14] the expression *castella caimitica*. (10) In spite of the metaphors arising out of the *prosopopoeia* there is a certain lack of pervasive figurative language, or any consistent use of rhetorical tropes and figures which we might easily find in the manuals. (11) Langland mixes Biblical material (John 8.44) with popular folk material in the connection of Judas's death with the elder tree without any suggestion of impropriety. Professor Bennett notes in the Holkham Bible (*c.* 1320-30)[15] that the tree is called *seur* in the Anglo-Norman text (55.4): 'se pendiit desure un seur', an expansion on Acts 1.18. Langland seems to have had a penchant for Anglo-Norman writings.[16] (12) Slight traces of colloquially loose grammar may be found in this passage towards the end. In line 68 there is a touch of reduplication in *sithen* ('then') and *after* ('afterwards'), though the final adverbial intensive is rhythmically effective. In line 69, the construction *lyeth hem* (where the verb is transitive) is not unknown to ME, but the Dictionary evidence does not suggest that the usage is literary.

All in all, I think the stylistic range of these lines can be called characteristic of Langland's artistic method. It lacks, of course, the lyrically heightened poesis of Passus XVIII, the more pointed satiric meiosis of the passages of social and moral criticism and the extensive display or injection of Latin quotation (mainly Vulgate) indulged in elsewhere in the text. Given these reservations, if we were to analyze the style of the *Gawain*-poet or any of the anonymous poets usually connected with the alliterative verse of Langland's day, we should arrive at entirely distinct attributes as regards metaphor, personification, formulaic repetition, use of connectives, rhythmic pace and conversational flexibility.

After Langland's original use of the *visio* form, the next important adaptation lies in the poet's handling of *allegoresis*. Rosemary Woolf has drawn attention to the 'unmedieval' way in which Langland uses allegorical modes in connection with the systematic or unsystematic construction of the *narratio*. In the disconnected, digressive satiric manipulation of personification and allegory an obvious parallel between Langland and Jean de Meun may be drawn. Their shared mentality is worlds away from Guillaume de Lorris or Alan of Lille. But Jean's allegorical technique is more sustained than Langland's in that there is a constant element of the poet's enjoyment of openly parodying the *education amoureuse* framework and milieu established by Guillaume. Self-conscious burlesque and extended ironies play an important part in holding the narrative and allegorical direction together. This is brilliantly highlighted by the subversive colloquy between Amors and 'Guillaume de Lorris' and the hardly-to-be-permitted-to speak 'Jean de Meun', set in an imaginary past before the poem has actually been composed. Amors lays down the plan of the work (*Roman* 10493-10680) with a majestic disregard for authorial feeling or sensibility. This passage lays the foundation for the poet Geoffrey Chaucer's exchanges with the God of Love and his Queen Alceste in the Prologue to the *Legend of Good Women*.[17] At the same time, Jean is more sustainedly digressive than Langland in that the *excursus* themselves are more continuous and tend to form quasi-philosophical or satiric *digressiones* which simply pursue their own direction and exhaust their topics before allowing the narrative force to return to the task of taking up what is left of the main plot-line, if that can be remembered. The long passages of *sermocinatio* and general conversational garrulousness of Jean de Meun are marked by a certain *esprit de raillerie* which recalls the self-consciousness of Byron in

Don Juan. The element of *tour de force* is as pronounced as is the quality of discursiveness. It does not matter who is speaking or whence come the voices, Jean de Meun has one style for everyone, including himself. Here and there in the *Roman* one can find passages which remind us of Langland—often when the narrative is slightly blended with *descriptio loci* (*Roman* 10057-10076), the self-description of a vice (*Roman* 11037-11082, of *Faux Semblant*). More often satiric treatment of the ecclesiastical life recalls Langland's sallies in that direction. Compare the interpolation after line 11222 delivered by *Faux Semblant*, an exposé of the cunning of friars:[18]

> Ainsi de vous esploitera
> Ja pour proiere nou laira,
> Ne pour defaute de deniers
> Qu'assez en a en ses greniers;
> Car Chevance est ses seneschauz,
> Qui d'aquerre est ardenz et chauz,
> Et Pourchaz ses freres germains,
> Qui n'est pas de pourchacier meins
> Curieus, mais trop plus d'assez,
> Pour quoi il a tant amassez,
> Pour ce est il si haut montez
> Que toutz autres a seurmontez.

This might be rendered into ME as follows:

> So stronge wol he worche þe þat for no prayere wol he halt,
> Ne for no pinche of pense—þerof pondes hath he ynough
> Garnered in a garret, of golde motouns an hepe;
> For Chevesaunce hath he chose as Chef Steward
> Þat in þaquist beth ardent,—aquite wol he neuere.
> And Porchace his brether, 'bi burthe' said he boldlye,
> Þat namore less takeþ tene for þe tailende
> Bot more þe merrier his golde þus tamassen,
> Þat mountyng so heigh al þe reume most surmounteþ.

However lamely this resembles Langland, the observations and the personifications could remind us of Langland's targets and angle of vision. But apart from these occasional overlapping of interests, the artistic methods cease quickly to resemble each other in Jean and Langland. Langland employs the allegorical more variously and more obliquely than his forerunners or contemporaries. In allegoresis there is the same darting, unsustained movement we can observe in his invention of the *narratio*.

The extent of Langland's splitting up of the allegorical process and translation of similitude into various planes and dimensions is so total and multiform that it has become almost imposible to categorize and classify the poetic types of allegory. And because allegoresis actually does not have the status of an 'art of expression' in Langland— because of the poet's almost intuitive grasp of the technique, close to, if not identical with actual compositional thinking, only the most obvious of the allegorical methods can be usefully identified. This state of Æsopic, fable-like flexibility, a continuous series of '*métaphorphoses évanescentes*.[19] has unfortunately turned the poem into a happy hunting-ground for Biblical exegetes (the 'new Puritans of Princeton')[20], and, in England, a tendency to categorize: personification allegory, dramatic allegory, diagrammatic allegory, non-visual allegory, exemplary allegory. However useful some of these categories, I think a later observation of Professor Salter and Professor Pearsall is nearer the secret of Langland's imaginative plasticity when they assert: 'The essential structure of his thought is figural ...' (*Piers Plowman*, York Medieval Texts, 1967, p. 27).

One comes to suspect that there is an element of deliberate mystification involved in Langland's invention of a variety of allegorical referentiality and the flexibility of allegorical perspectives and planes of allusion. Part of the poet's pursuit of the creating of suspension and uncertainty keeps the ostensible quest for 'Truth' afloat, hovering just out of intellectual reach. But an aesthetic problem, unfortunately comes into play with the creation of mystification: since there is no sustained normative form either at the level of interpretative 'symbolism' or narrative sequence, the reader's intelligence tends to abandon the search for 'connections' as well as the search for 'unity'—or our minds turn to an amalgam of all the possible 'schools' of criticism which can be used to lend coherence to the parts of the poem.[21]

The range of the poet's allegorical references can be simple or very complex. At its most simple we see Langland using conventional signpost allegory. In Passus V, Piers the pilgrim gives a guide to 'Treuthes dwelling place'. The allegorical map is not original with Langland but he has been taken to task for inventing allegories such as:

Þe mote is of Mercy þe manere aboute,
And alle þe wallis ben of witte to holden Wille oute ...

(V. 595-6)

Now, we can see the function of 'tenor' and 'vehicle' in the 'walls of
Intelligence' but the proper function of the virtue 'mercy' is to open,
enlarge, admit. It is a liberating virtue. The function of a moat is to
exclude entry. It is a defensive architectural feature. Professor Bennett's defence of this image is not entirely convincing. He argues: 'the
meeting-place rather than the boundary between the Old Law and the
New, for Mercy is shown to those who keep God's commandments
(cf. Exod. 20:6)'. But we are not being asked to imagine meeting-
places or boundaries, much less Laws. The simple fact is that Reason
has begun by preaching to a huge audience ('Alle þe reume to
preche') and what Piers has before him is a heterogeneous multitude.
The dramatic context requires a simple, basic use of conventional
signs and language (we know what happened to Henry James when
he tried to inquire his way to the Bath road). Thus, Piers exploits imagery shared by Grosseteste's *Casteau d'Amour*, a *Sermon* of St
Augustine and Frere Laurent's *Somme le Roi* where the moat
represents such unlikely virtues as Charity and Humility.[22] The
aesthetic determination of the sign-post allegory derives from the
dramatic context of the poem. At the other end of the scale, a few lines
further on we come across a passage which requires a great deal of
elucidation:

Per Euam cunctis clausa est, et per Mariam virginem patefacta est;
For [s]he hath þe keye and þe clicket þouȝ þe kynge slepe.
And if grace graunte þe to go in in þis wise,
Þou shalt see in þiselue Treuthe sitte in þine herte
In a cheyne of charyte, as þow a childe were ...

(613-16)

This complex of imagery has been brought together from various
texts, all of them implying 'interpretations'. The C-Text clarifies
Langland's meaning but ruins the allusiveness of the imagery. Professor Bennett rightly sees the womb/lock/key/virginity nexus in the
Advent liturgy blended with John 14.17 and Matthew 18.3. I think
the 'cheyne' is undoubtedly a chain of office and has no real connection with philosophical chains of love (*Roman* and Boethius, *De Cons*.2.
m.8). It comes to Langland from a more popular source, the blessing
given with the kiss of Peace in the *Breviary* (Sarum Rite): 'Habete vin-

culum caritatis et pacis ut apti sitis sacrosanctis misteriis'. This was all uncovered years ago by Miss Hanna who deserves to be acknowledged.[23] Admittedly, a person with ecclesiastical training amongst Reason's multitude would find this splendid and moving poetic compounding more immediately available. But its intensity and complexity of compounding of separate elements shows Langland's ability to construct condensed and complex 'allegory' with a positive tangle of associations, none of them irrelevant. Consider the suggestiveness of 'kyng' and 'slepe', the possible ambiguity in *þow* (= ? þou3), where both the perceiver into the heart and the figure of 'Truth' can (and ought) to be children, or as if children (compare Passus XV. 145ff.).

There are three main characteristics of the poet's use of the allegorical, however simple or complex in referential density. The first is his insistent recourse to the process of personifying. Langland preserves and extends one of the main origins or sources of the allegorical activity as it evolved from Classical and Late Antique literature,—but with the essential difference that the poet increases rather than diminishes the 'impure' nature of *prosopopoeia*. Prudentius in the *Psychomachia* or Alan in the *Anticlaudianus* IX keep only the barest essentials of the reality factor, thereby tending to reduce the reader's involvement in the allegorical action. Every element tends to become more abstract. Their poetry becomes a clever exercise and the 'events' lost their particularity. Langland, on the other hand, instinctively dramatizes and enlarges the elements of reality, pushing the personifying activity closer and closer to its roots in actual human activity. The elements become more and more concrete. The association with common life and its institutions are multiplied and made more actual or concrete. He has the same genius for this type of invention as Ovid had. There is an intense topicality in all of Langland's allegoresis. He effortlessly puts his allegorical creations in a concrete place. The second characteristic of his allegorical art is the poet's love of sententiousness. He not only has recourse to frequent *sententiæ* but the author constantly intrudes in a moralizing way into his allegorical dimensions, expounding or extrapolating either briefly or at length. There is both strength and weakness in this activity, and often it seems as if the author has taken us further into an examination of a problem than the literary moment or context requires. Langland's indulgence in sententiousness often contributes to the digressive nature of the narrative rhythm. The author seems unaware of the structural subversiveness caused by his habit of moralizing and

expounding. The third element provides a source of some strength for
Langland's narrative continuity. This is Langland's penchant for the
parabolic mode. In common with all medieval writers, Langland has
constant recourse to *parabolæ*[24], but in addition he has a tendency to
see separate episodes as shaped in a moral and parabolic way. Thus,
the 'fable' of the rats and the cat (Prologue 146-207) is not really a
fable, but is more like a parable: it has precise and pointed moral and
political application, though the author tries also to maintain its open-
endedness of fable texture. But its exact application is called attention
to by the poet's open and deliberate (and fearful) refusal to indulge in
any interpretation: 'Deuine ȝe, for I ne dar, bi der God in heuene!'
The exemplary or parabolic use of the fable of the rats and cat was
popular with preachers and poets. Nicholas Bozon used it in the fourteenth century[25] and Eustache Deschamps wrote a ballade on the
same subject (probably not read by Langland). Bishop Thomas Brin-
ton introduced the fable into a sermon that he preached before king
and parliament on 17 May, 1377. But the rat of renown and the
mouse who knew what was good for him are Langland's own inventions. The poet's contemporary audience was invited to make certain,
unmistakable, identifications. Gower's allusion in *Vox Clamantis* I.vi.
493ff. points in the same direction. One is invited to see the rats as
lords temporal or knights of the shires; the mice could be identified as
members of parliament or simply the burgess members drawn from
the merchant classes. The cat suggests the powerful John of Gaunt.
The reference to 'cullying' ('killing') in line 185 indicates that a more
severe action had been contemplated beyond 'belling'. There had
been an attempt on the life of John of Gaunt in 1377. The Rat of
Renown (lls. 158ff.) should be identified with Peter de la Mare who
had been spokesman in the 'Good' parliament for the reddress of
grievances (and had been arrested and imprisoned in Nottingham).
Professor Bennett sees that line 160 'suggests he is speaking from the
viewpoint of Westminster'. Line 206: 'Coupled and uncoupled' suits
the political context by alluding to the joint or separate power of
Gaunt and Richard II. All of the imagery in this passage points to a
topical understanding, whether we like it or not. Although the
parabolic mode is introduced suddenly, with no transition (an
attention-catching device), the fable connects with the main plot-line
in that line 207, the last line of the 'fable' ('Forþi vche a wise wiȝte I
warne wite wel his owne') repeats and emphasizes line 122: 'eche man

to knowe his owne', one of the main moral duties. What appears perhaps to be *laissez-faire* will be given a scriptural basis in Passus VI.

In spite of the inherent tendency of the phraseological element in alliterative composition to throw up types of conventional idiom and a stock of grammatical formulations and repetitions of key-items, there is not much in Langland that is conventionally 'poetic'. If we compare recurring words and phrases in the other West Midlands poems written in alliterative lines, there cannot be above a dozen words and phrases which *Piers Plowman* shares with them, The main reason for this, I believe, is Langland's original status as a writer and his limited reading experience of what we would classify as 'literature'. His quotations and allusions come from other more pragmatic, quarters. Another reason for Langland's lack of verbal reminiscence springs from his instinctive desire to reach a wider audience, though not necessarily a more popular audience. His concern for what the nineteenth century was to call 'the condition of England' requires a national width of reference—and his poetic language answers perfectly to that challenge. On the whole, if we look at the poet's topology, he seems to take up a 'metropolitan' position. Most of Langland's references to places concern London and include actual streets and buildings. Outside 'Troy Novant', Langland seems to know the northwest and west better than the south and southeast. Oxford and Cambridge go unmentioned (unlike Chaucer). The closest he gets to Oxford is Abingdon (and that by way of the abbot). Everything lies within about 150 miles of St Paul's (with the exception of Chester in V. 467, but this may only turn out to be the appropriate citation in an oath).

Langland's poetic language seems to indicate a close contact with colloquial speech, or at least gives the impression of a certain colloquiality. A striking formulation involving tropological invention is the compressed *comparatio* incorporating alliterative pairing. We find the following type of expression which displays vividness of observation combined with the suggestion of current ordinary usage:

'naked as a nedle' (XII. 162, XVII. 56).
'as doumbe as deth' (X. 137).
'as hore as an hawthorne' (XVI. 173).[26]

This type of expression is fairly frequent and calls attention to the poet's ability to create memorable commonplaces. Skeat commented that 'naked as a nedle' may be a proverbial expression, though examples are not that plentiful; 'as doume as deth' is parallelled by the very common 'as dombe as stone' and the not quite as common 'dombe as a doornail', but the dictionary evidence suggests that Langland's phrase may not be proverbial; 'as hore as an hawthorne' is parallelled in one fourteenth-century lyric *Open a somer soneday se I þe sonne*—a poem Langland almost certainly knew—by the phrase 'hor als hore-howne', where the comparison is with the herb white horehound. Langland's use of the massed hawthorn blossom is much more memorable and realistic. Guillaume de Lorris had written in the *Roman* of Vieillesse (346-7):

Toute sa teste estoit chanue
Et blanche con s'il fust florie

but there is no particularization of tree or shrub to compare with Langland's succinct visual crystalization of phrase and natural observation.

In larger narrative units and paragraphs Langland is fond of antithetical constructions and patterns (a habit perhaps encouraged by his reading of the medieval satirists in Latin and Old French). So, too, his usual poetic language as reflected in verbal detail exhibits a remarkably consistent creation of contrastive qualities. The famous phraseology in the Prologue: 'toure on a toft / depe dale binethe' provides a basic paradigm for Langland's use of contrastive images. The poet seems to exploit little deliberate poetic or rhetorical shading. There is hardly any colouring which brings into play graduating effects. His language has little 'timbre'—the effect is like that of medieval musical instruments (especially the *fidula*), vibratoless and slightly sharp. In eliminating the principle of gradation, contrastiveness collapses rhetorical perspective and much of the usual stylishness traditionally associated with 'ornatus'. An editor's notes tend to take the reader back into fourteenth-century reality or account for some figurative transformation of the actual. The figural and the actual are closely linked together. Larger units reflect the contrastive mode: we find habitual use of comparative groups of personifications, motives or moral judgments. Lines 42 ff. amplify the core expression:

'Fayteden for here fode / fou3ten atte ale;'

The dominant poetic qualities are the result of a connection-impelled condensing in which the concrete and the figurative extension are forced together, not one element being led out of the other by a process of gradual unfolding. Langland's imagination seems to work through a mixture of compounding and association. There are few traditional extended similitudes or metaphors. When he attempts an extended *allegoria* it usually takes the form of a schematic construction with a somewhat laboured symmetry. Professors Salter and Pearsall call this type of schematic invention, 'diagrammatic allegory'.[27] In the case of Dowel, Dobet and Dobest, the basis is a somewhat old-fashioned 'grammatical metaphor'[28] which creates an anomalous category of adverb-verb compound (modelled on later Latin *benefacio*) used as a noun and compared as an adverb or adjective. There is a vast grammatical metaphor added by Langland in the C-Text[29]. Skeat had to admit that he thought it was Langland's invention but he disliked it and thought it boring. But there are exceptions. In Passus V. 136-142 Wrath describes himself:

'I am Wrath', quod he, 'I was sumetyme a frere,
And þe couentes gardyner for to graffe ympes;
On limitoures and listres lesynges I ymped,
Tyl þei bere leues of low speche lordes to plese,
And siþen þei blosmed obrode in boure to here shriftes.
And is fallen þerof a frute, þat folke han wel leuere.
Schewen her schriftes to hem þan shryue hem to her persones.'

The description begins seemingly illogically (a gardener would have been a lay office), unless we understand that Wrath once was temporarily a friar far in the past and now, more recently, has become a gardener (compare the shifting, Protean series of disguises for *Faux Semblant* in the *Roman* which includes being a friar). But the botanical imagery is logically progressive (grafting, first growth, blossoming, bearing fruit), connected and developed (*low speche, obrode*). A creeping plant with runners, much resembling strawberries (a frequent symbol of humility) is insinuated into the reader's mind. The similitude dissolves finally into a moralizing observation and abstraction. There is considerable literary skill shown here, a skill which Jean de Meun would have admired and appreciated (cf. *Roman* 11187 ff.).

Of the schematic type of allegory, one of the best examples is the long agricultural similitude of Passus XIX. 257-315 which substantiates the office of Plowman in its spitirual and moral labour. The interplay of 'tenor' and 'vehicle' is sustained reasonably well, though one wishes that the poet had used more specific terminology (*hoe, pyke, mattock, rake, twibil*) instead of repeating the general noun *harrow* for the separate cultivating activities. In lines 307-8 'loue' is imagined as some sort of plant that is encouraged to grow 'amonge the foure virtues and vices destroye'. Agriculturally this is difficult to imagine: some kind of unrecorded arable ground-cover? The agricultural allegory does not end here but moves on to the construction of a *granarium*. The materials donated by Grace become openly improbable and the allegorical texture or mode reverts to the sign-post simplicity of Passus V in the relationship of tenor and vehicle. This is as close as Langland approaches to the imaginative amalgams of Bunyan. We experience force and clarity in the poet's writing here, but it seems to me that the verse has lost its allusive texture and its quality of spontaneous compression, its succinctness. The poet is now in a mood of expansion and schematization. Langland's real poetic strength lies in figural compression. This conjunction of one image with another in a brief, simple, swift verbal movement recalls Coleridge's remark on Bunyan's ability to perform the same type of invention: '... the power of the predominant idea (that true mental kaleidoscope with the richly coloured glass) on every object brought before the eye of the mind through its medium.'[30] That medium in Langland is the economy of instruction, the *modus didactivus*. In his *Table Talk* Coleridge characterizes Bunyan's prose style as 'the lowest English, but without slang or vulgarity'. He further says that if one were to refine it or add anything 'literary' in the accepted sense, the composition would be destroyed. Langland's style has a similar didactic efficacy which typifies its best compositional vitality. The writer is assiduous in finding similar qualities in preaching, satire, biblical text, scriptural commentary and a range of visual Christian images and symbols.

No doubt Langland found 'authority' for some of the tendencies of his verse composition in Scripture, although one would resist a claim that his search arose from a systematic or philosophically rigorous adaption of sacred 'invention' along the lines of, say, Dante or St Augustine. He would have taken comfort in St Augustine's justification of figurative invention in sacred writings and he would have found imagery and intensity of expression in the prophetic books. One fears he may have found in St Jerome justification for the extended use of *digressio* - but the recourse to digressions was widespread in medieval taste generally in any case.[31] I have reserved for the last, some account of Langland's love of action, of activity. Whatever Dowel, Dobest and Dobet may be taken to signify, the 'Do' element is the most important element in the grammatical metaphor. Langland's special sensitivity for verbs shows itself most strongly in passages of heightened lyrical intensity - and these passages are invariably concerned with the Incarnation and the Passion. Here the poet's lyrical emphasis seems to find a proper 'climate' for poetic transport or sublimity. But it is not just the verb *solo* which is memorable, the whole line and related phraseology is carried into memorableness along with the 'key item'. The following verbal inventions remain unforgettable and in some cases are brilliantly original. In Passus V. 486-517, Repentaunce's prayer anticipates the triumph of Passus XVIII. The Passion of Christ engenders lines of a startling lyric intensity and energy:

> þe sonne for sorwe þerof les syȝte for a tyme
> Aboute mydday, whan most liȝte is and meletyme of seintes;
> Feddest with þi fresche blode owre forfadres in darknesse;
>   *Populus qui ambulabat in tenebris, vidit lucem magnam;*
> And thorw þe liȝte þat lepe oute of þe Lucifer was blent,
> And blew alle þi blissed into þe blisse of paradise.

>   (V. 499-503)

Professor Bennett's valuable notes explain the complexity of the compounding of sources of imagery here, and their devotional richness of emphasis. Yet the vigorous and original verb *blewe* in line 503 troubled him. After much speculation (including 'scribal anticipation') and the weighing of alternatives ('*drewe*: cf xvii. 117 ...'), he finally admitted: 'On the other hand, it is Christ's *breath* that breaks hellgate at xviii. 319.' The final evidence for *blewe* lies in lines 514-15 where Hope seizes a horn:

> , þanne hent Hope an horne of *deus, tu conuersus viuificabis nos*
> And blew it with *Beati quorum remisse sunt iniquitates,*
> þat alle seyntes in heuene songen at ones...

Whatever the origin of the horn (the Easter *Exsultet* or the horn of salvation in Psalm 17.3), the rejoicing looks forward to Passus XVIII, to the pipe of Peace and the Tromp of Truth (407, 422):

> Treuth tromped þo and songe '*Te deum laudamus*'

These culminating celebrations all have Easter orientations. The metaphoric activity in the active verb *blewe* is not just local but looks forward to the futurity of the key Passus in the whole poem. Shortly after the celebrations for Easter (accompanied by the pealing of church bells: 'rongen to the resurexion'), the dreamer *ipse* commands:

> 'Ariseth and reuerenceth goddes ressurrexion
> And crepeth to þe crosse on knees and kisseth it for a iuwel.'
>
> (427-8) [fol. 81b]

The imperative verbs 'creep' and 'kiss' have the same memorable power and are grounded in the actual ceremony of penance associated with Good Friday, though, as Skeat commented, the ceremony was not always associated with Good Friday. The Everyman editor sees the shadow of penance still reflected in the dreamer's injunction, an acknowledgement of human participation in 'the suffering that made that victory possible'. But the tone here is of rejoicing and Langland may also have had in mind the injunction in Vulgate Psalm 68.35: 'Laudent illum caeli et terra, mare et *omnia repentia* in eis', 'Let the heaven and earth praise him, the seas and everything that creepeth therein'. In this same category of usage we remember 'love leaping out of heaven' (XII. 141) and the strangely powerful:

> [Riche men rutte tho and in here reste were
> Tho it schon to the schepherdes a shower of blisse.]
>
> (XII. 152-3)

Here the primitive, echoic verb *rutte* ('snored') is thrown into abrupt contrastive emphasis against the 'shower of blisse', shining for the waking and vigilant shepherds, where the noun 'shower' is a complex and sophisticated poetic compounding. It combines several meanings and a host of associations: (a) 'a showing example', with reference to (1) the angel, 'the glory of the lord' (Luke 2.9 and Lydgate, *Lyf of Our Lady* III. 460-469), and (2) the star of Bethlehem (cf. B-Text, XVIII. 231 ff.); (b) 'a shower', as of rain, compare Psalm 71 (Vulgate) 'Et descendet sicut pluuias in vellus, et sicut guttæ stillantes super terram', and (more importantly), Isaiah 45.8: 'Rorate caeli, desuper, et nubes pluant iustum', an image selected by both Deschamps and Dunbar for their poems on Christ's nativity:

> *Rorate celi desuper*
> Hevins distill ʒour balmy schouris...

As Professor Ross comments: 'The opening line is both a recollection of the liturgy of the Advent season, and of the Officium of the Mass on the Feast of the Annunciation'.[32] Lydgate, too, did not forget this crucial text in his *Lyfe of Our Lady* III. 631 ff.:

Spake Ysaye, and sayde in wordes playne:
'The high hevynes doth your grace adewe,
And sayde also: the skyes sholde reyne
Vpon erthe, her moystur for to shewe;
And bad the grovnde, eke in wordes fewe,
For to open and thorowe his heuenely showre,
For to buryovne our alther savyour.

How much more compressed and succinctly memorable are Langland's two lines in Passus XII. It is suitable witness to his conviction-impelled vitality of figural and realistic compression.

CHAPTER FOUR

Satire

There's Wrath who has learnt every trick of guerilla warfare,
The shamming dead, the night-raid, the feinted retreat;
Envy their brilliant pamphleteer, to lying
        As husband true,
Expert impersonator and linguist, proud of his power
        To hoodwink sentries.
Gluttony living alone, austerer than us,
Big simple Greed, Acedia famed with them all
For her stamina, keeping the outposts, and somewhere Lust
        With his sapper's skill,
Muttering to his fuses in a tunnel "Could I meet here with Love,
        I would hug her to death."
           W. H. Auden, *Which Side Am I Supposed To Be On?*

The modern poet's lines are effective for they revert in these stanzas to the older medieval mode of personification, the simple schema of the Seven Deadly Sins, the application of technique and moral idea to our strangely resistive modern circumstances. The rhythm utilized is basically Poundian (especially the 'hell cantos') and although the alliteration has been repressed in Auden (more so than in Pound), the distant Langlandian original can be faintly heard in some lines and half-lines:

Expert impersonator and linguist, proud of his power

Gluttony living alone, austerer than us

The original pattern in Pound derived from a reading of Langland's *Piers Plowman* (as the poet once admitted) and we still hear echoes in Auden's lines. But the modern poet's effectiveness lies precisely in consciously regressing to an earlier critical mode safe in the assurance that the reader will feel the archaic, unexpected energy—for reader and poet have experienced the long emergence of Classical 'formal satire', its naturalization, cultivation and extension over the period from Wyatt's adaptations of Alamanni to the eighteenth century and its subtle modulation of all the Latin satirists into the balancing cultivation and urbanity of the Horatian and the Ovidian. Our notion of the 'satiric' (apart from mere vituperation) has become wedded in the educated reader's mind with the procedures (superficially more polite than crude) and refinements which originated in the naturalization of Horace, Juvenal and Persius. There is a conscious shock when the poet of our own days reverts to a style of satirizing which was superseded by that of the neo-Classical. Our sensibilities receive a similar shock when Dr Faustus in Marlowe's play is delighted by the recitation of the Seven Deadly Sins. They sound old-fashioned and crude, more like Langland than anything choice and Renaissance. Faustus has the mind of Gabriel Harvey!

The modern poet and the Renaissance poets shared a luck denied to the medieval poets in that the medieval writer interested in composing satiric verses had none of the sixteenth- and post-sixteenth-century critical scholarship, richness of commentaries or imitations in the vernaculars of the great Roman poets. Unless he was remarkably learned, he could not have read Quintilian's survey[1] or understood much of the original texts of Horace or Juvenal with any set of reliable notes to hand. He might have consulted Horace's remarks in the *Ars Poetica* and whatever material he could have pieced together from Vincent of Beauvais. If he had consulted that favourite of encyclopaedias, Isidore's *Etymologiæ* he would have got a very queer idea of the nature of satire—a kitchen-sink definition: anything and everything goes! It is a receipe for licence not poetry.[2]

Satyrici autem dicti, siue quod pleni sint omni facundia:
sive a saturitate et copia.

The manuals of rhetoric do not help much; the descriptions are brief, reasonably ill-informed and detailed technical advice conspicuously lacking. Imitations were restricted to medieval Latin and Old French. The original models (if they deserve the name) seem to have been distantly appreciated, if at all. Some poets, such as Walter of Chatillon, took to satire instinctively and produced amusing, nipping poems of a more personal and distinctive kind. Others merely became crude and indulged in the loudly vituperative, such as Serlo of Wilton. In John of Salisbury we have a polished exponent of formal satire; in Bernard of the *De Contemptu Mundi* we read a barbarous and long-winded exponent of abuse.[3] But the well-spring of medieval inspiration for satire or satirical writing was by and large local and, although Walter of Chatillon's verses founded a 'school', the main bulk of French and English Latin satiric writing in the twelfth century was not immediately carried over into vernacular adaptations or imitations.

The satire which we can trace to Langland's reading lies in the less sophisticated adaptations in Huon de Meri's *Le Tournoiement de l'Antichrist* and the ecclesiastical *Devil's Letter* in Latin and Anglo-Norman which give rise to the wonderful, satiric marriage-contract in Passus II.[4] The A-Text of *Piers Plowman* was completed and the B-Text underway before Gower had embarked on the *Vox Clamantis*. Broadly speaking, Langland's satiric field of vision looks back to the general satire, the *Satura Communis* of Henry of Huntingdon (*fl.* 1084-1155) where the victims belong to all the estates of the realm and the display of vices is large and generalized. The commonly held view that the *persona* of the satiric poet in the Middle Ages is wholly anonymous and democratic is not entirely true. John of Salisbury and Walter of Chatillon *inter alios* cannot be so described. But the presence of a strongly indicated individual person and the complex interplay of personality and *persona* in the actual poetry are not widely practiced in Medieval Latin or vernacular satire. We need only look for a moment at this kind and degree of complexity of invention in Horace, admirably analysized by Professor Durling,[5] to grasp what Langland could never have easily read or appreciated. Only in Chaucer and Deschamps is the satiric and ironic manipulation of persona-directed nuance systematically and dextrously exploited.

But even here, Langland's originality comes to his aid in satiric inventions. The sustained intensity of vividness of the poet's passages of satiric writing are the product of the same religious conviction which lies behind the lyricism of the religious creations of Passus V and Passus XVIII. What *indignatio* was to Juvenal, *persuasio* or *bileve* is to Langland. In both authors a mode of the grimly humourous comes into being. In Juvenal the observations are less generous and *meiosis* or diminishing becomes the poet's sharpest and most frequent poetic and satiric practice. Langland's satire always distinguishes between the sinful or misguided person and the sin admonished—he has more respect for individual 'souls' than had Juvenal. Langland's favourite device lies in the 'reality' of the image, its exhibitedness, what the grammarians called *praesentatio*. Compare the sad note of implied compassion transmitted in this vivid rendering of slothfulness:

And þanne to sitten and soupen til slepe hem assaille,
And breden as burghswyn and bedden hem esily
Tyl sleuth and slepe slyken his sides;
And þanne wanhope to awake hym so, with no wille to amende,
For he leueth be lost—þis is here last ende.

(II. 96-100)

Professor Bennett observes that these lines are parenthetical and no part of the 'charter' proper: 'The poet is carried away by his detestation of gluttony.' It begins in abhorrence but ends in something less censorious, I believe. Moral forbearance apart, Langland was able to imagine one ironical dimension which helps to create a kind of distance between the personality of the waking poet-figure and the dreaming poet-figure: the discrepancy between the dreaming author's *bileve* in activity, the performance of good works, and the waking poet-figure's recurring life of idleness and lack of social engagement: 'And ȝede forth lyke a lorel al my lyf-time'. Sometimes the waking and dreaming roles are reversed. The important events of Passus XVIII press upon the poet's consciousness and he instantly writes down his experience: 'Thus I awaked and wrote what I had dreamed'. Yet, though he hurries off to church to celebrate Mass (in honour of the Redemption he has just witnessed), he quickly falls asleep before he can take communion. One can justify the artistic necessity for the movement into a prolongation of the poetic transmission of vital religious experience, but the occasion reflects strangely on the worthiness or unworthiness of the persona. Beyond this single ironic plane, Langland creates no complex dimensions of irony and moral perspective for his persona—at least of the kind native to the art of Horace.

But however grim the vein of humor, there is hardly an instance of identifiable *caricatura* in Langland's satiric presentation, little that can be attributed to some stylistic rendering or mannerism. If the object viewed by the poet appears 'distorted', he usually manages to convey the impression that it is the vice which has already caused the distortion, not the medium of poetic rendering. He approaches somewhat near Dante in this respect, though without Dante's systematic raison d'être. Pound in his 'hell cantos' can imagine little beyond images of disgust, images of ordure, decay and unnaturalness—and there is no humour, not even of incongruity. Langland never 'insults over' viciousness (as did Persius) or 'condescends' (Juvenal), postures frequently adopted by all Renaissance satirists including Donne. Horace hardly ever loses his equanimity, as the person who is the writer, whatever loss of temper occurs in the character of the writer in a given dramatic context. But unlike Horace, Langland never makes the object satirized look absurd or ridiculous, much less (like Juvenal) ridicules abuses directly. As Langland never seems to strive after an effect (he is, as an earlier critic noted, 'veracious in his simplicity') so he always appears conservative and orthodox in the estimation which has arrived at the act of *reprehensio*. There is always a 'text', an authority, eminently reasonable, within easy reach. And the poet often reaches after the Latin, not only as a *justificatio* but also as an impulse to go on to a related or new topic.

The mode of the satiric is rarely dealt with as a separate element in Langland's literary composition by any of the poet's modern critics or editors.[6] This seems odd, especially if we turn to the early and carefully produced Bodley MS. Laud Misc. 581. Great care has been taken over the format of the book, rubrics, headings, underlinings, punctuation, paragraphing and correcting. Built into the format or *ordinatio* of the manuscript book is a feature inherited from the exemplar which the scriptorium and their text scribe and flourishers thought important enough to reproduce as an intrinsic visual characteristic of the text. This feature is the *nota* signs (often overlaid in red) included in the book production at the copying stage and at the 'finishing stage'. These signs are not 'scribbles' or 'additions' to the text, they are an important part of the book's original display format. If we tend not to notice them it is because editors (with modern ideas) have not recorded them and because they have become rubbed and faint as a result of the handling of the leaves. When the book was new they were much more arresting visually. There are seven major *nota* signs and we can see at once where contemporary or near-contemporary interest lay:

(1)   fol. 1b. the fable of the rats is marked *nota* in the hand of the text scribe.

(2)   fol. 19a. 'On limitores and listres lesynges I ymped' (V. 138) is marked *nota* in the hand of the rubricator or flourisher.

(3)   fol. 30a. 'Thorough flods and þourgh foule wederes frutes schal faille' to the end of Passus VI. 326ff. is marked *nota* in the text hand and is overlaid by the flourisher.

(4)   fol. 47b. 'Ac moche more in metynge þus with me gan one

dispute' (XI. 316ff.) is marked *nota* in the hand of the text scribe and paragraphed by the flourisher.

(5) fol. 56a. 'My wafres þere were gesen whan *chichestre* was maire' (XIII. 271) is marked *nota* in the hand of the rubricator or flourisher.

(6) fol. 60a. 'whan *constentyn* of curteysye holykirke dowed' (XV. 519ff.); passage 519-523 is marked *nota* in the hand of the text scribe.

(7) fol. 91a. 'One frere flaterere is phisicience and surgiene' (XX. 313) is marked *nota* in the hand of the rubricator or flourisher.

There are no *nota* signs against any of the specifically religious or lyrical or allegorical passages. The significant areas inherited from the exemplar, an earlier circulated book, which became part of the format of the Laud book are concerned with secular affairs: the parabolic fable of the rats, the disreputable behaviour of friars, prophecy as history, the mayorality of Chicestre (1369-70), the donation of Constantine as poison of the true church, the sexuality of human beings. Many of the passages marked are in Langland's satirical mode, especially the 'fable' and the self-description of Wrath. 'Medieval' and 'Renaissance' interests in the poem are distinct then from modern preoccupations, at least in respect to this one important aspect of Langland's literary invention.

In this treatment of satire, I shall divide Langland's critical mode into three main headings: (1) objects of satire; (2) technique of satiric *præsentatio*; (3) the structural relation of satiric units to the main *narratio*. The chief problem concerning the objects of satire is the unlimited field of the poet's interest. Unlike neo-Classical satirists, Langland is not concerned to direct his criticisms at individuals (compare Skelton's obsession with Wolsey) or even fictionalized 'persons' or even *bona fide* aspects of individual behaviour which may have originated with the observation of 'individuals'. 'The poet is more conversant with the passions of mankind than with individuals' as one early reader of Langland put it. This atomization of satiric aims and objects goes back to the basic tendencies of the *Satura Communis*. As far as Langland is concerned, his main satiric techniques probably derived from his reading of the mid thirteenth-century satiric poem *Le Tournoiement de l'Antichrist* (after *c.* 1245) written by Huon de Meri. In his poem personification and personified viciousness behave very much in the manner of Langland. There is the same general tendency to combine and emphasize major and subordinate features with abstract properties deriving from one and the same source: a part or parts of a generalized moral nature of man. There are traces of Langland's actual reading of Huon in Passus XX. Like Jean de Meun, Huon's style is octosyllabic couplet and the verse details are quite unlike Langland. But there is more influence exerted on Langland than Skeat would allow. Huon's poem should perhaps not be considered entirely by itself—it is related to a group of poems heavily influenced by the *Satura Communis* tradition, the Old French 'Songe' form and the encapsulated militant oppositions, antitheses, and contrastiveness derived ultimately from Prudentius's *Psychomachia*. Huon cites Raoul de Houdanc's *Songe d'Enfer* and there is a later poem, *Le Tournoiement d'Enfer* written after *c.* 1285 which borrows from Huon and perhaps from Jean de Meun. All these poems show similar satiric deployment of *topoi*: cities, feasts, military or chivalric groupings, contests etc., which reflect simple poetic structures: antithesis and contrastive emphasis, balancing of scenes. The later *Tournoiement d'Enfer* is abstract and conversational in style. Raoul, the elder poet, is down-to-earth and mocks various nations and states in an amusing off-hand way. But in Huon we find a more imagistically concrete style of satiric exposé which (apart from the obvious borrowing in Passus XX) suggests the fundamental origins of satiric specificality in Langland. Compare the satiric account of dish and sauces in Passus XIII. 43ff. with the following description of one of the infernal courses at the table of Antichrist:

> Fors tant qu'un entremet i ot
> D'une merveilleuse friture
> De péchiés fais contre nature
> Flatiz en la sause cartaine.[7]

This might be rendered into ME alliterative verse as follows:

> Douȝty was þentremet, daintilich serued,
> A merveil made at Castel-Bordel of moustring friture,
> Farced with fele synnes, *decoctus contra naturam*,
> By capital culpes was the coke ycrouned;
> The friture walwed in gilt wawes depe wellinge
> Of sewes of Charteres, sop who-so lykes.

Although the octosyllabic line suggests none of Langland's verbal arrangement, yet the vivid reality of the imagery, its metaphoric com-

ponents, and its compressed allusiveness through word-play and pun
(*flatir/flater*; *cartaine*: 'Chartrean'/money minted at Chartres) would
have appealed to Langland's creative satiric sense. Huon's style is
meandering and monotonous but occasionally he produces this order
of concentrated, memorable satiric gem. Langland, since he read the
poem, could hardly have missed it. In Langland the realisation of this
technique becomes typical of his intuition of the possibility of immediate satiric exposure by means of day-to-day human activities,
commonplace but arresting morally and poetically, continuous short-
hand, compressed concretizations. Jean de Meun (who also borrowed
from Huon) saw the same possibilities in Huon and the generic relation to Ovid and Alan. Langland saw the exploitable connection between Huon and reality itself. Once acquired as a satiric technique, it
affords Langland the finding of endless possibilities for transforming
ordinary medieval reality, all manner of activities and visual material
and material objects into satiric exemplifications which may resemble
similar depictions in other poets (Ovid often springs to mind). Yet
Langland's method possesses an innate ordinariness of diction quite
unlike the stylistic contrivances of Ovid's distichs and hexameters.
The diction is as ordinary as the material being transformed, subject
and medium are closely matched. Even the 'locking' device of
alliteration recalls colloquial habits of pairing phraseology rather than
the more stiff formulations of the authors of other alliterative poems
containing social criticism.

Langland's habitual satiric stylistic register raises two related problems. First, the ubiquitousness, range and endless flexibility and ex-
pansiveness of the satiric mood is not entirely Langland's invention.[8]
This has been transmitted from the *Satura Communis* via the Old
French imitators. Secondly, Langland's poetic diction is almost
entirely free from stylistic concerns which may be related to the usage
of rhetoric - the 'ornatus' of the manuals and the practice of learned
poets. In grammar and syntax, too, Langland seems liberated from
the 'poetic' concerns arising out of Old French couplet rimes or the
intricate syntactical variations employed in medieval Latin leonine
verses. The style of *Piers Plowman* has an admirable freedom of movement and development, but at the expense of a counterbalancing normative artfulness. Both these artistic concerns, the general scope and
the stylistic means of creating 'targets' lead Langland into endless
incrementations and additions. The controls of Roman formal satire
are absent. The prevailing general freedom of satiric invention helps

to promote a lack of controlled expectation and hence contributes to the impression of formlessness.

When we turn to the three main aspects of satire mentioned before (object, specific technique and relation to satiric *topos* to *narratio*), the reader often finds it hard to define the distribution of satiric emphasis in the poem according to the reasons already outlined. But however difficult it may be to locate the poet's distribution of satiric emphasis and its relation to the *narratio* in any given Passus, yet the critic must persist in trying to perform a structural analysis. Certain key constructional patterns emerge. Let us look at the Prologue and Passus I to VII in the B-Text as a complete poetic unit.

The Prologue is the most clearly structured book unit as regards the distribution of satiric emphasis. Langland's method is progressive, the satiric mode gradually saturating the main narrative until the *narratio* is entirely subsumed by the satiric force. The stages are clearly marked and the reader is left in no doubt about 'meaning' and mode of presentation. The *exordium* and the *conclusio* are differentiated by poetic mood and technical handling from the main flow of the *narratio*, and where the aural and visual emphasis is pronounced. The *exordium* (lines 1-10) technically is a *chronographia* which defines the pre-sleep *præfatio*, deliberately mellifluous in sound and rhythm, deliberately allusive, reminding the reader of the *exordia* of other, older alliterative poems and obliquely reminding him of Psalm 22 (Vulgate);

> Dominus pascit me, et nihil mihi deerit.
> In loco pascuæ ibi me collocauit.
> Super aquam refectionis educauit me.

This unit (1-10) is in some manuscripts bordered in a box, sometimes in the flourisher's red, sometimes in the same ink as the text hand. It is deliberately isolated from the rest of the text. The dream narrative begins with a universal *descriptio loci* (Malvern belongs to the waking world), earth, heaven and hell, concentrating naturally on one of the recurring and focusing images of the poem 'a faire felde ful of folke'. As the *narratio* changes its descriptive emphasis into an account of activity (*pragmatographia*) it introduces the various estates and occupations ('condiciounes') of medieval society. This last category changes the descriptive emphasis into an enumeration by congeries (there is no systematic classification) which becomes progressively more and more satiric - by line 34 the dominant mood is wholly satiric and critical. The author's interest varies with the groups. Some exemplary groups are given more extended treatment; the pardoner, bishops and university-trained clerks are given more expansive exposé. The abbreviatory expression of line 110 breaks the progress of the satiric mood and Langland seems to revert to a more neutral tone as the *enumeratio* starts again with the king and the secular court. But the poet has only beguiled us for a moment, for he introduces into this group the first personification of an abstraction, innate moral sense (line 114). The presence of Kynde Witte serves as an artistic catalysis - the introspective 'eche man to knowe his owne' engenders a sudden transitional passage, pageant-like in imagery, allusive and secretive in conveying puissant political dilemma and message. In terms of fourteenth-century consciousness there was probably a strong connection between the *angelus aureus* of the pageant presented before Richard II the day previous to his coronation and the sermon (containing the fable of the rats and cat) preached by the bishop of Rochester on the day after the coronation. But the political colouring as regards the relation of king, the commons and the law calls into being the central episode in the Passus, the fable of the rats and cat (a *digressio*) which occupies lines 146-207. Langland embarks on this central digression without any transitional verses at all. It is as if 'þe commune' of line 143 of normal size and shape were suddenly metamorphosed into the rodent 'communes' come together to discuss their 'commune profit'. The fable itself demonstrates Langland's instinctive understanding of the potential and actual range of the devices of the beast fable, not least its practical wisdom: 'For better is a little losse þan a longe sorowe' (195) or the extensive use of naturalistic *sermocinatio*. With the practical, proverbial redefinition of the philosophical formulation of line 122, the fable ends as suddenly as it began, marked by a two line *exclamatio* which calls attention to the necessity for the reader to find the appropriate interpretation. The author dares provide none. Immediately the poet returns to the enumeration by congeries which characterized his former satiric method. The beginning again with the serjeants-at-arms and the law-courts is connective, as Professor Bennett noted. The groups show no categorization by rank, though the tendency is to move downward into 'craftes' (221) and we end with a miscellaneous assortment of navvies, cooks, cooks' assistants and Inn keepers.

The *conclusio* (lines 222-230) is one of the most poetically evocative of Langland's creations. It shows his 'dissolving technique' at its most effective. The Prologue drifts away into pure sound, echoes of street cries, partially song and incantation. These are basically the cries of Eastcheap (in Candlewick Street ward) not too distant from Langland's Cornhill ward. Some are recorded in the anonymous late fifteenth-century poem *London Lickpenny*. John Stowe summarises: 'in Eastcheape the cooks cried hot ribs of beef roasted, pies well baked, and other victuals; there was clattering of pewter-pots, harp, pipe and sawtry ... some sang of Jenkin and Julian ...'[9] The cries are themselves 'echoes' in so far as Langland's verse formulation must have distorted them in some degree. The fourteenth-century lyric *The Land of Cockayne* (line 104) records the collocation 'gees, al hote, al hote'. At least three English musicians (Gibbons, Weelkes, Dering) wrote musical settings for the text of 'The Cries of London'. The type of formulation 'hote pies hot' is represented in the later text by 'Hot mutton pies hot'. Unfortunately, the text does not record any cries advertising wines. The Old French evidence provided by Guillaume de Villeneuve's poem *Les Crieries de Paris* (written *c.* 1290)[10] does not help much on wines. There is only one cry recorded (124-5): 'Le bon vin fort a trente doux'. There are similar types of repetition: Farine pilée, farine' (145), 'Chaus pastez, chaus gastiaus' (62). Interestingly, the phrase: 'Dieux vous doinst santé' (26) forms part of an actual street cry. Hence, in Langland, the navvies' work-song 'Dieu vous saue, dame Emme' is probably helping to form a transition into the vending cries which directly follow. I cannot agree with the editors of the York Medieval Texts that there is a pointed reference to gluttony in this passage or that the *conclusio* is in the least part of the allegory. The editors compare the conclusion to the end of section II of Eliot's *Waste Land*. Eliot's use of sardonic conversation is far too satiric and far too symbolically pointed. Pope uses descending, shortening echoes to end book I of the *Dunciad*, but this use, too, contains satiric reference, not least to the 'bog-house'. Langland's *conclusio* moves away from *significationes* back to the ordinary, concrete reality out of which the satiric sense of place and society had been originally created. The cries and songs are the echoes of that ordinary reality of 'Middle Earth'. It reminds me of a line in Carlos Williams's poem *Lear*: 'Like smoke from bonfires blowing away'. One wishes that Langland had not written the last line (230): 'Al þis seiȝ I sleping, and seuene sythes more', but it may be argued that the phrase 'seuene sythes' is an oblique attempt to call our attention to the seven Passus to follow, thereby indicating the integral nature of this part of the B-Text. But the same words, it should be noted, are retained in the C-Text where this postulated numerical pointing will not work.

Passus I shows a complete redistribution of satiric emphasis. With the change in the dreamer's status (from spectator to interlocutor and participant) the dominant mode alters from the satiric to the didactic. The entrance into the dialogue of an august personification (Holy Church) does much to eliminate the satiric and ironic, though Holy Church does not spare human nature and society her criticisms. Shorn of nearly all satiric emphasis, Passus I suggests that Langland is distantly reflecting the contrastive, antithetical narrative movement of his models in Old French and medieval Latin. Perhaps he alerts the reader, too, for the same, reverberatory rhythm is to emerge in Passus II. This Passus maintains the narrative continuity and immediately introduces the famous portrait of Lady Meed whose *effictio* is accomplished entirely in terms of her clothing and jewellery (lines 23-4 of the Prologue are deliberately recalled). Holy Church's account of her 'background' consists of a mixture of realism, didactic criticism and petulant invective. Theology will shortly give a less biased account of her origins in lines 114ff. Holy Church moves into anger and vituperation through dramatization but none of this can be called satire.

Satire enters the moment Holy Church leaves. Without any significant transition, Langland engages on the *topos* of the spousal of Meed (her engagement, not her wedding) which has satiric antecedants in the *Roman de Fauvel* and elsewhere. To this *topos* Langland engrafts the Anglo-Norman and medieval Latin parody excursions into the *Epistola Luciferi* which is here adjusted so that the document serves as a spiritual charter and a settlement contract. This parody form is skilfully interwoven with narrative elements and authorial commentary. The decision at line 153ff. to embark on a journey to London to have the contract with Fals tested at law in Westminster generates another satiric *topos*, 'the parade of the vices', but wonderfully changed and extended. Part of the poet's impulse doubtless derived from his memory of Nicholas Bozon's *Le Char d'Orgueil* (where allegorical animals are depicted drawing carts) for behind the *Epistola Luciferi* lurks Bozon's poetic epistle *Sir Orguylle li Emperour*. Langland was later to take other touches from Bozon's *La Chanson de la Passion* (for some aspects of the Four Daughters of God) and Bozon also provided the sources of the depicting of *humana natura* on Christ's 'helm' and 'hauberk'. Langland's freedom of treatment of the old notion of sins mounted on appropriate beasts, distinguishes his satiric method from the *significationes* orientation of the traditional *topos*. Here the animals

are not in the least exotique or symbolic. They are realistic, domestic
beasts of burden who basically remain untransformed into beasts.
The vicious pack-animals remain human. The combination is far
more degrading: 'a shryreue shadde al newe', 'a sisoure þat softlich
trotted', 'a flaterere fetislich atired'. Perhaps Langland had also
remembered illustrations (compellingly vivid) of 'Aristotle ... whom
that the queen of Grece so hath bridled' (Gower, *Confessio Amantis*
VIII. 2707).

The 'parade' *topos*, firmly anchored in the narrative movement as
the journey to London, is terminated by the king's decision to 'at-
tache þo tyrauntz' (199), 'to arrest those ruffians'. The procession
breaks up into a rabble, warned by Drede, dispersing and vanishing
into the stinking back lanes of London and the remotest corners of the
shires. The *conclusio* of Passus II (lines 210-236) again shows
Langland's penchant for 'dissolving techniques'. There is a parallel
with the transformation into sounds at the end of the Prologue. Here
the figures of Falsenesse, Gyle and Lyer are shown being transformed
by various disguises into cover occupations and false sanctuary. Lyer
attracts the main satiric emphasis: he is shown undergoing a dazzling
series of Protean transformations[11] - a novitiate pardoner, a clyster-
gazing physician, a crooked apothecary, a minstrel, a government
messenger, and finally an 'unlimited' friar.

After this concentrated series of grafted-together satiric *topoi* of
Passus II, the narrative line of Passus III and IV is relatively free of
such concentrated satiric emphasis. The 'attachment' of Meed is
presented through a medium basically 'realistic' in texture, though
there are occasional deviations into irony and satiric distortion. Some
of these miniature satiric excursions are successful (III. 35-36), mainly because of the shading of 'personification allegory' into satiric
nuance; some are not satisfactory (III. 65-86) owing to Langland's
inability to resist personal didactic intrusion in the 'action'. Professor
Bennett excuses III. 76-86 on the grounds that these lines must represent an officious scribe's intrusion, or a fragment of a larger episodic
discourse that was missing from, or never completed in, the '*Ur*-text'.
I think this is just Langland being carried away on the wings of
sententious interpretation ever-widening. The C-Text (which ex-
pands even further) may be part of the mood of empassioned
digressiveness. Once back on course, the rejection of Meed by Conscience is openly critical and the personification-realism easily accom-
modates satiric and ironic textures. Even Lady Meed indulges in

ironic castigation when she attributes the failure of Edward's 1359
Normandy compaign to the behaviour of Conscience. Her point, one
supposes, was that the winter campaign was blessed by the native
church. The secular preparations were well-undertaken (the army
was well-provisioned and the famine in the area had been thoroughly
investigated). But the weather was terrible, as Meed testifies in an
unforgettable line (190): '[þow] crope into a kaban for colde of þi
nailles'[12].

The main alllegorical action involving Meed presses forward in
Passus IV but the plot-line is suddenly interrupted by a long digression in which Pees presents a 'bill' against Wrong (lines 47ff.). One
feels that the poet has lost interest in exposing Meed or has used up all
his evidence. There is a passage of direct didactic satire in Reson's list
of *impossibilia* (lines 113-133) but the Meed narrative progress gets
sidetracked. Her 'conditional discharge' seems to end the king's
preoccupation with her, however restricted her actions may be in the
future. The working agreement between the crown, Reson and Conscience (a verbal agreement on personal oaths) provides rather a weak
conclusio for the Passus and what, after all, had been a main narrative
interest from the beginning of Passus II.

Passus V has no narrative connection with the previous Passus,
whatever the linking moral concerns. In the C-Text the break is even
more pronounced in that the poet or an editor wakes the dreamer up
and produces a long and fascinating 'biographical' account. Further,
the dreamer wakes up in London (in Cornhill ward) which sorts oddly
with his having fallen asleep on the Malvern Hills. The writer of the
C-Text is perfectly aware of this and mentions the place where the vision began. No inconsistency is apparently seen. The B-Text breaking of the narrative is much more economically managed (lines 3-8)
and is dovetailed into the new setting (a national sermon, a *sermo ad
status*, by a dream church). I do not think the dreamer is meant to be
imagined as 'in a more devout frame of mind'. The waking/going to
sleep device is merely a mechanical indication of the narrative discon-
tinuity and gives the vision a fresh impulse. The ME verb 'babel' is
not neutral and we should not try to read too much into his saying his
'creed'. The grammar makes it plain that the saying of the 'Ave' or
'Pater Noster' helps to induce hypnotically the sleeping state (he is
already faint from lack of sleep, lines 5-6). The 'babbling on beads'
perhaps may indicate the degree of 'wo' (line 3) in the poet's mind as
a consequence of not having 'sleped sadder and yseiȝen more'—a

symptom of spiritual unrest. The remedy *in slepe* is near at hand ('saw I moche more') and the poet is returned immediately to the 'kirke' he had already seen distantly in his previous dream. But I do not think the sermon is preached inside the church. We are outside in 'þe felde ful of folke' with a huge audience ('alle þe reume'). It is the mainly Dominican habit of field preaching that is being drawn on here. The cross which Reason brings to preach before suggests a special moment, a crusade or a pilgrimage—and pilgrimage 'to seke Treuthe' (519) is what the audience (still out-of-doors in lines 520-21) embarks on.

After the relatively satireless Passus III and IV, Passus V is composed largely of the major satirical portraits of the Seven Deadly Sins, with original and selective treatment. The occasion of confessing is not intended to be serious; it is simply an excuse for vivid, satiric self-presentations. As before observed, Langland normally has no recourse to open caricature as part of his satiric technique, mainly because of the poet's deliberate aim at realistic appearance in the presentation and his underlying generosity towards persons as ultimately reformable. But in the confession of the 'sins' there is no residual aspect of these personifications which contains a reformable person. Persons are not represented. Sins cannot repent, though they may be imagined as going through the motions of confessing. Hence, the selected sins as self-presenting 'characters' in Passus V show a high degree of visual distortion or caricature. Their rather more devious internal moral states do not cause as much surprise—I suppose because external appearance is more carefully regulated in our behaviour than the unseen irregularities of our mental life. Biology is more conservative than psychology. Langland's imagination shows much alteration in the changing of details in the portraits 'from recension to recension'. But this degree of variation need not reopen the question of multiple authorship. The satiric freedom made possible by the permission of a greater direct use of satiric distortion naturally stimulates the authorial imagination to change the emphatic texture in response to local personal pressure we can no longer trace or discover. In the imagining of the self-presenting sins we discover instead the instinctive self of Langland responding selectively towards objects of the most recent and nearest moral detestation, a sort of splenetic holiday.

In any case, in all versions certain human transgressions seem to strike no answering chord in Langland's concern for reformation or desire for satiric exhibition. These areas, one must suppose, represent aspects of human misbehaviour where the vice as practiced has less tendency to damage the functioning of social groups or social inter-relationships. Pride and Lust are hardly touched by Langland and are certainly given no special imaginative treatment. They announce themselves merely to make up the traditional members of the vicious family. Perhaps they should be thought of as malpractices most damaging to individuals and least corrupting as regards 'society'. It has been observed that the poet is hardly indebted to any particular version of the presentation of the seven capital sins in medieval literature. In an area where the reader might well expect a dependence on literary and/or iconographical schematization, one receives instead a highly original invention, almost a *jeu d'esprit*, but one which recalls in copiousness and *esprit* the garrulous energy and delight in minute satiric observation worthy of Jean de Meun more than it evokes parallels in other verbal accounts or visual analogues. The satiric impress comes direct and clear from reality passed quickly and strongly through the poet's imagination. Intermediary 'sources' or carrier traditions are automatically eliminated. There is an iden-tifiable rushing in of unmediated reality, reflected in the high in-cidence of names, Christian, surnominal and place-names: Peronelle (160), Sir Henry (189)[13], Symme-atte-Stile (201), Wy (205), Wyn-chestre (205), Walsingham (230), Bromeholme (231), a long list of Christian names with alliterating occupational surnames (315 ff.), Cockeslane (319), Garlekehithe (324) etc.

The element of visual distortion or caricature yields an impressive array of particularizing details and vivid poetic phrases: 'pale as a pelet' (78), 'as a leke hadde yleye longe in the sunne'[14] (82), 'nyuelynge with the nose and his nekke hangynge' (135), 'And made hem joutes of iangelynge' (158), 'as a lethern purs lolled his chekes' (192), 'al bislabberd, with two slymy eizen' (392). Avarice's loose coat cannot be forgot:

And in a tauny tabarde of twelue wynter age,
Al totorne and baudy and ful of lys crepynge;
But if þat a lous couthe haue lopen þe bettre,
She shoulde nouzte haue walked on þat welsche, so was it
thredebare.

(V. 196-199)

The Cornhill district was noted for its stalls devoted to the selling of second-hand articles of clothing of rather poor quality.[15]

The portrait of Accidia ends the satiric dimension of the Passus at line 468. Lines 469-84 represent a deliberate transitional episode. Editors have not agreed about the relation of this passage to the main narrative progress. I do not think the figure of 'Robert þe robbere' represents an 'eighth sin', nor is he a continuation of the 'confessional scheme'. He looks forward to other important ideas (Langland is fond of forms of anticipation) but his chief function here is to introduce a new focus and to provide an excuse for the author himself to interpose a concluding verse paragraph (479-484) which further distances the major satiric excursus in the Passus. Langland can then return to the original social context of Reason's sermon and the wider, national audience. The 'hem' of line 455 is not specifically directed at the sinful but to the 'reume' of the *sermo ad status*. The tone of the poetry changes radically into a new seriousness and lyricism. This new seriousness continues until we reach the very end of the Passus when brief snatches of conversation follow on the heels of Piers's instructional address, voices which glance at another collection of the potentially unworthy, 'a cutpurs', 'a wafrestre', 'a pardonere', 'a comune woman'. The poet ends by commenting wryly: 'I ne wot where þei bicome'. This repeats his observation on 'Robert þe robbere' of lines 479-84. The transitional passage of 469-84 indicates Langland's awareness that a sudden antithetical juxtaposition of the satiric excursus and the intense religious lyricism of lines 484-519, lines which anticipate the whole of Passus XVIII, would have been poetically awkward. The C-Text interposes an even longer didactic and admonitory passage in the authorial voice (material originally used in the B-Text at Passus XIII. 410-57).

Although Professor Bennett believed that 'I ne wot where þei bicame' signalled that 'these characters are now out of the story' (p. 196), the miscellaneous groups of wastrels of a similar blood-sucking variety are soon to reappear in the very next passus. In Passus VI the 'mixt allegorical' scene of the half-acre soon gives way to Piers' critical observations (119 ff.) on the quality of his labour force. This gives rise to a general satiric description of the types of wastrel activity which Piers finds himself supervising. Soon it is clear that Langland means to exploit his 'dissolving' or 'melting' technique in this Passus. The *descriptio* quickly modulates into a series of conversations and disputes which in its turn rapidly generates an allegorical action involving the personification of Hunger. About line 215 ff. the satiric colouring gives way to the fused satiric-didactic. Then the satiric-didactic melts away into an admonition which dissolves into a dark prophesy, sinister and ill-boding. These lines have never been successfully explained:

> Ac I warne ȝow, werkemen, wynneth while ȝe mowe,
> For Hunger hiderward hasteth hym faste,
> He shal awake with water wastoures to chaste.
> Ar fyue ȝere be fulfilled suche famyn shal aryse,
> Thorwgh flodes and þourgh foule wederes frutes shul faille.
> And so sayde Saturne, and sent ȝow to warne:
> 'Whan ȝe se þe sonne amys and two monkes hedes,
> And a mayde haue þe maistrie and multiplied bi eight,
> Þanne shal Deth withdrawe and Derthe be iustice
> And Dawe þe dyker deye for hunger'—
> But if God of his goodnesse graunt vs a trewe.

(VI. 322-332)

I have departed from previous editorial punctuation and placed the whole of the prophecy in the mouth of Saturn. The punctuation of Mr Schmidt is already moving in this direction. The last line belongs, alone, to the poet-figure. To my mind, the context (a warning delivered from the planets) suggests an astrological application whereby the 'mayde' of line 329 might be interpreted as the constellation sign of Virgo (August time and hence appropriate for the harvest season) and 'maistrie' might suggest the astrological sense of 'dominance'. The phrase 'multiplied bi eight' seems impenetrable. The force must be mathematical not alchemical. I suspect it simply means eight Augusts hence, leaving no exact date in the reader's mind for the prophecy is not intended to be fulfilled—compare the equally vague 'fyue ȝere' line 325—much less properly understood except as a condemnation of slothfulness, deceit and greed. Why the author should wish to address the labouring classes indirectly through a warning wrapped up in a prophecy is difficult to fathom, unless he wishes to create an atmosphere of forboding, an ominousness which is meant to forshadow catastrophe on the scale of the coming of Antichrist in Passus XX. Skeat believed that the poet deliberately introduced an element of ridicule in the passage, a debunking of the mode of contemporary prophecies. This explanation would save the poet's reasonableness at the expense of a grim humour which seems to have as little purpose as the introduction of the prophecy itself—unless this is the only kind of warning which a labourer might heed ('I can speke lewedly to a lewed man').

But the essence of the popular prophecy lies in its irrationally bringing into the present a future which behaves as if it already had the power to be true, if only we could understand its words, the secret of its message. This Saturnian prophecy contains an unsolveable sequence of imagery and so attains all the fascination of a riddle, but the final end of the prophecy is severe; 'death' may withdraw but the workman will die anyway. The prediction is not a riddle but a curse. There is an aesthetic properness in the severity of the foreboding and its being placed in the mouth of Saturn. Like the *conclusio* of the Prologue, the melting and dissolving techniques finally transform themselves into words, mere sounds, part riddle and part malediction. The final, mollifying words of the poet seem to hold out only the slenderest thread of hope.

The special, oblique use of an amalgam of parodistic forms in Passus VII banishes the satiric mode almost completely from this Passus. The special position of the poet-figure not only as narrator-character but unfolder and interpreter of the 'subtext' document (called a 'pardoun') sent to Piers also helps to eliminate any recourse to satiric invention. This crucial 'subtext' is composed of a blend of at least three types of communication: (1) an ecclesiastical pardon; (2) a royal pardon; (3) the literary invention called 'the charter of Christ.[16] As Rosemary Woolf has convincingly argued,[17] the documentary 'subtext' is unfolded to us in a curious way. From line 4 onwards the poet-dreamer acts as an omniscient interpreter and often translator of the pardon of Truth, going through the imaginary document clause by clause. The poet's intellectual and emotional involvement is intense and the tone urgent. But it is as if we were being taken through the fine print of the pardon—we never see the opening formulae or its main statement of intent. Dramatically, the poet depicts himself as standing just behind Piers and the Priest when the 'bille' is at last opened—though the poet-figure has been interpreting and expounding the document for more than 100 lines. The imaginary amalgam of two types of pardon and the charter of Christ dissolves before our eyes. The written leaf contains but two lines consisting of clause 40 of the Athanasian Creed. What follows has engendered much interpretation (too much one is tempted to say). It is as if the personal basis of the dreamer's intellectual anticipation of the 'pardon' remains either fictive or imaginative, incapable of eventually being guaranteed by an institutional aspect of the Church, or formal written documents emanating from any social institution. But the dramatic invention, the poet's retreat into deliberate ambiguities of dream experience and the authorial trust in the real efficacy of good works, as well as the firm identification of Dowel with Christ (199) provides the Prologue and seven Passus unit with a convincing concluding rhythm. The satiric intrudes here only for a brief moment: 'I sete ȝoure patentes and ȝoure pardounz at one pies hele' (194) revives in a brief flicker the poet's sharp tongue and eye—whatever a *pies hele* or *pye-hele* may mean.[18]

CHAPTER FIVE

Langland's Christ

Ex quo plane sequitur quod ille homo sit homo, sicut ille homo est Deus-homo. Nam Christus et Deus-homo convertuntur simpliciter et ex equo: et per consequens, sicut conceditur quod Christus est Christus, sic concedi debet quod Deus-homo est Deus-homo.
John Wycliff, *De Benedicta Incarnatione*, cap. iv.

It is striking enough that Wycliff should have appropriated St Anselm's famous paradoxical compound 'Deus-homo' (and all that implies), but the appropriation is further complicated by Wycliff's Augustinian conviction (recorded in chapter iii of the *De Incarnatione*) that the Christ who descends into hell and liberates the souls confined there is not an angel or pure soul. He appears to the demons and the prisoners in the person in which he suffered temptation and physical pain—but not death. The Incarnation was not interrupted by death. The harrowing of hell is the action of a person. This exults man, humanity, above the status of angels. Christ as a man ruled in earth, hell and heaven. Yet equally striking are the plain words in the above passage: 'simpliciter et ex equo', 'simply and equally'. There is nothing complicated theologically in this 'conversion', and the equality of God-man, Christ and man is absolute and clear.

In like manner, Langland's clarity and simplicity on the Atonement cannot be questioned, but the poet does not follow Wycliff concerning the 'person' who appears in hell. Passus XVIII. 259: 'a spirit speketh to helle', line 304: 'a soule cometh hiderward seyllyng ... God it is', and Christ's own words (364): 'I deyde vpon erthe' indicate Langland's position. But on the Anselmian paradox conveyed by the compound *Deus-homo*, 'God-man' Langland and Wycliff are in substantial agreement; Langland preserves the full meaning of the original Anselmian idea. The crucial passage is contained in Passus XI. 192-203 in Trajan's long speech; these lines expand on an earlier statement made in Passus VI. 210:

'In þe olde lawe, as holy lettre telleth,
"Mennes sones" men called vs vchone,
Of Adames issue and Eue, ay til god-man deyde;
And after his ressurreccioun *Redemptor* was his name,
And we his bretheren, þourgh hym ybouȝt, bothe riche and pore.'
                                                        (XI. 192-6)
                                                        [fol. 46a]

Langland is the only Middle English writer to use the Anselmian
compound 'God-man'. The *MED* (*God* 4a.) merely records
Langland's unique compounding but makes no special comment on
the origin of the expression. The *OED* does not record the compound
until the mid sixteenth century, and this usage is stated to be the
translation of an ecclesiastical Greek compound θέανδρος (undated).
But Langland's unique use of the compound must descend ultimately
from Anslem's famous coinage in the treatise *Cur Deus-Homo*. In the
C-Text Passus IV, 404-6, in the long grammatical similitude,
Langland anticipates the Anselmian compound earlier:

> For that ilke lordes loue that for oure loue deyde
> And coueited oure kynde and be cald in oure name, *Deus-homo*
> And nymen hym unto oure number, now and euere more;

The reason for Anselm's linguistic creation reflects directly on
Langland's emphatic and crucial repetition of the text of Romans
13.7: *Reddite ergo omnibus debita* (Passus V. 469) and Matthew 18.28:
Redde quod debes (Passus XIX. 177-193). As Dr. Evans once explained
concerning the origin of the idea of the *Deus-homo*:

> The God-man is the only solution of the paradoxical demands of
> the human situation. Only man ought to pay the penalty for sin,
> but he cannot. Only god can pay, but He ought not. Only God-
> man both owes and is able to pay the debt.[1]

The conditional nature of the act of payment (that man in return
gives his love to God and to his neighbour) is intrinsic to the Pardon-
Charter formulation of the 'Charter of Christ' as it evolves in the first
quarter of the fourteenth century onwards.[2] Langland is plainly at-
tracted by the imagery of payment, pardon and legal contract (the
origins appear to lie in St Ambrose's *Commentary on Luke* 23, and
Hebrews 9.15-18, especially the phrase 'Testamentum enim in mor-
tuis confirmatum est ...', where *testamentum* blends the sense of 'last

will' with a new covenant ('Et ideo novi testamenti mediator est ...')
promising an eternal inheritance), perhaps because the reality of this
imagery brings the mystery of the atonement within the range of
medieval learning and understanding. So, too, Langland in Passus
XI. 196 insists that our inherited brotherhood is 'quasi modo geniti and
gentil men vche one' and again in Passus XVIII.22: 'This Iesus of his
gentrice wole Iuste in Piers armes'. This relates to another popular
medieval notion, namely that a secred heraldry asserts that Christ was
of noble birth: '... of whom that Gentleman Jhesus was borne, very
God and Man ...'[3]. The original Biblical expression of Christ's
lineage and its embodiment in the arbor vitæ is given an everyday application. The Incarnation is also included in the range of medieval
ordinary understanding. This concretizes and clarifies the original
passage in Romans 8.17 as expanded and glossed by Nicolas de Lyra
(Glossa Ordinaria VI. 107 and 113). In all of Langland's poetic
treatments the poet is shown reducing and conflating without becoming in the least idiosyncratic. The sacred heraldry and 'Prynce of
Cote-Armoure' is effortlessly grafted on to the imagery which
Langland remembered from Bozon's La chanson de la Passion:

> La ventaile de l'hauberk estoit la face bele
> Qe privément en chambre lascera la pucele.

The figure of Christ in humana natura seems to concentrate and focus
the poet's poetic creativeness: image-clusters form associative se-
quences of sustained lyrical resonance which convey dramatically and
immediately the central significance of all of Christ's activities. We
acknowledge without hesitation the rightness of the poet's impulses:
for example, the dramatic placing of the debate of the four daughters
of God between the crucifixion and the resurrection as a prelude and
witness to the harrowing of hell. Langland means here to stress the
power not the potentiality of Christ's atonement (compare Lydgate's
treatment in the Lyf of Our Lady for the more conventional placing of
the debate in potentiality). Langland is not entirely original here. He
is indebted to Bernard and Grosseteste for the emphatic placing.[4]
Still, the language and the whole dramatic sequence of Passus XVIII
belongs to the poet alone, whatever analogues and parallels we can
adduce.

   There are three related moments of the passion in Piers Plowman
which form the apex and axis of the poem: Passus I. 150 ff., Passus V.
472 ff., and Passus XVIII. Each moment shows an increasing interior

complexity and lengthening of poetic development. Constellated round the three moments are the lesser and plainly subordinated recapitulations of Christ's life and works. At another distance, subordinated further by oblique rather than direct application, are the symbolic elaborations or allegorical cross-referencings which either image forth Christ-like identifications or generate special quasi-pictorial elaborations of Christ-bearing significance, such as the Tree of Patience in Passus XVI.[5] The habit of turning images this way and that, recombining material, anticipating and repeating is deeply instinctive with Langland and not unconnected with his constant revising of his own writing: 'its author could never let it alone, nor less could his copyists'. Why Langland should have wished to anticipate the dramatic sequence of Passus XVIII by the Tree of Patience episode of Passus XVI seems a little mysterious. The emphasis in XVI plainly falls on the personal and psychological aspect of the hypostatic union. The York Medieval Text editors see the Tree episode as 'a plateau, preparing assault on the just visible peak of Christ's sacrifice by mapping and displaying the terrain'. There is a comparison made with *Purgatorio* XXIX. 43 which I do not understand. The York editors are right, I think, to say that 'the style of the allegory here is formal, pictorial and numerological, a method of explaining and informing, not of persuading'.[6] It is certainly not logical or argumentative. At the same time it is not devotional either: it lacks depth, concentration and calm. In fact, it is 'formal and pictorial' only up to a point. In the C-Text version, the Tree of Charity (the version which concerns the York Text editors) there is more excuse for viewing the allegory as formal and pictorial for the texture of presentation has been made prosaic and the dream context removed entirely.

The dream context of the B-Text helps to explain the reason for the appearance of the Tree of Patience episode and helps to account for the peculiar style of the quasi-allegorical elaboration. There is a pre-sleep mis-en-scène which establishes by rethorical *partitio* the schematic nature of the imagery and the 'imposed allegorical' nature of the dreamer's recognition of the relation of physical image to *significatio*. The sign/signifier system is basically statemental: Mercy is the root; the trunk is ruth; the leaves are loyal words ('the law of Holy Church', Langland feels constrained to add); the blossoms are Obedient Speech and Kind Countenance. The whole tree is called Patience; the fruit is Charity. This imposed allegorical series of identifications is then expanded by an application to physiology: the garden in which it grows is the human body; humanity is the root-stock (implying that the tree is a grafted fruiter); the arbor of the garden is the human heart and Free Will is the tenant farmer who does the physical tending of the tree for Piers Plowman. Some of the particulars overlap and some are merely elaborated. There is nothing, as yet particularly striking in this defining adaption of arboreal iconology (Augustinian in origin). But the mention of Piers's name causes a deep alteration in the poet-figure's emotions. 'Al for pure ioye' he swoons. The ensuing dream is not the result of fatigue or lack of food or sleep or any of Langland's usual mechanical excuses. It is the result of sensibility heightened to ecstasy. The dream does not come at once and the dreamer has no mental picture of definiteness, no unconscious companions. The language is peculiar here; the poet uses an adjective unique in ME, *lone*.[7]

And laye longe in a lone dreme and atte laste me þouȝte
þat Pieres þe Plowman al þe place me shewed...

[fol. 69a]

When Langland finally is released from his lengthy solitude of dream suspension it is Piers who is his only guide and companion. Now the imposed allegorical elaborations cease to be defining, becoming instead more and more complicated and less logical. The substance of the arboreal dream becomes a spectacular fantastical display, full of activity and dramatic floridity of style. The death of Christ ends the dream and the poet awakes, his eyes surcharged with tears (line 167). The peculiar, illogical flamboyancy of the developing imagery is the result of the personal, psychological state of the ecstatic poet-dreamer. There is little that is 'old-fashioned' or 'medieval' about the episode and its arboreal preoccupations. It has closer connections with the extravagances of Viennese *art nouveau* or the cinematic confections of Ken Russell. It almost transcends bad taste, or perhaps has nothing to do with taste. The episode's actual connection with the main narrative direction is no longer of any importance for the episode has become a personal, emotional excursus, florid and self-indulgent. The dreamer-poet (under Piers's direction) sees the arboreal detail eagerly and clearly ('I perceyued it sone'). The *significationes*-full tree develops additional complications. It is difficult to convey the mass of superimposed detail without extensive summary of the material. Briefly, the Tree of Patience has three props for sustaining its branches (the power of God the Father, the wisdom of God the Father, and the third prop is unidentified in the B-Text; the C-Text names it as the Holy Spirit). The props protect the tree from three winds (the world, the flesh and the devil). The tree is threatened by various diseases which attack the blossoms and the fruit (the main canker being Covetousness). It also suffers from wind-rock, the hostile incursions of unkind neighbours, brawlers and chiders. Some of these are thrown up into the tree; others (presumably) mount by means of a ladder whose rungs are composed of lies. The defence is chiefly in the hands of Free Will (with the help of Grace and the Holy Spirit). Free Will strikes at the devil with the third prop and is successful ('thus haue I the maystrie').[8] Hardly has the reader digested this bewildering amalgam of *significationes* than there is a transition made to an inquiry into the nature of the green wood which composes the props. The poet moves on to a related arboreal elaboration. The props, of course, are made of one tree (the Trinity) which grows in goodness. The tree also fruits (of various kinds: Matrimony, Continence and Virginity). Quite without adequate reason or plausible motivation, the dreamer asks Piers to pluck down an apple so that he can taste it. Why should he wish to? Widowhood and Matrimony weep and grieve and a host of apples come raining down. Why should they, he only asked for one? The fallen apples are the souls of the Hebrew Just Men from Adam to John the Baptist. The devil steals the apple-souls and stores them away in his infernal larder. Piers strikes out with one prop, 'Filius' ('for pure tene', the phrase recalls the tearing of the Pardon in Passus VII), and then with the 'grant of the Father' and the gift of the Holy Spirit he goes to 'rob' the devil and take back the fruit. After this gallimaufry of arboreal similitudes and imposed 'meanings', the narrative changes texture at lines 90 ff. and we are taken into a more settled gospel-based account of the life and Passion of Christ. Much of the elaboration of the arboreal imagery is not properly logical and often contradictory. Many of the *significationes* are unconvincing and some elements defy the finding of explicable equivalents. The passage is overfull of activity and mixes various modes without restraint or much regard for proportioned design or *dispositio*.

It is as if Langland required the intense and prolonged release of his personal emotions as a preparation for Passus XVIII: a deliberate exuberance bordering on the grotesque[9] as a method for acquiring artistic calmness and control. When we finally arrive at the *exordium* of Passus XVIII the narrator is penitent and exhausted, no longer mindful of the world or his physical condition. His dream of the Passion in Passus XVIII is preceded by no ecstatic condition:

> Wolleward and wet-shoed went I forth after,
> As a reccheles renke þat of no wo reccheth,
> And ȝede forth lyke a lorel al my lyf-tyme,
> Tyl I wex wery of þe worlde and wylned eft to slepe...

[fol. 76b]

If I have offered no aesthetic or literary explanation of the placing and development of the Tree of Patience episode in Passus XVI it is because I believe there to be no convincing aesthetic principle at work here. The poet's *inventio* has been signalled by the dream emotionalism to lie close to underlying psychological pressures and requirement at this point in the poet's involvement and the poem's evolution. The inwardness of the search in the vita (from Passus VIII onwards) encourages a closer psychological propinquity and hence the possibility of the release of personal emotions in a way in which the visio cannot so stimulate the author's mentality so directly. Of course I am offering no 'psychological theory' - pressures of the unconscious mind. Langland's expression of 'symptoms' only can be observed and these personal pressures relate directly to the act of 'dreaming' and composition.

The poet's first Christocentric passage occurs in Passus I. 150-172. Significantly, it is the simplest poetic treatment and it is the first of the three major passages. There is no preludic anticipation for our initial introduction to Langland's Christ, yet at the same time the image is not immediately that of a person - it is oblique and figurative, made up of compounded elements which begin in a botanical similitude. The 'plante of pees' is an adaptation of the 'tender plant' of the messianic text of Isaiah 53.2. That the plant could not be contained in heaven because of its weight and its desire to 'eat its fill' of earth is a bold and unique reversal of an image possibly taken from Vulgate Psalm 22.26 where 'the meek shall eat and be satisfied', 'Edent pauperes, et saturabuntur', (in its Augustinian interpretation) is not attributed to the Apostles, the eating to the Passion, but is here reapplied by Langland to Christ craving to be nourished by Incarnation,[10] and when so nortured 'of þis folde flesshe and blode taken' by a swift and audacious paradox then made wondrously light:

> And whan it haued of þis folde flesshe and blode taken
> Was neuere leef vpon lynde liȝter þerafter,

And portatyf and persant as þe poynt of a nedle,
That myȝte non armure it lette ne none heiȝ walles.

(I. 152-155)

The conventional ME expression 'leef vpon lynde' refers to the
Ascension (Professor Bennett aptly cites the use of the phrase in *The
Castle of Perseverance* in connection with the soul ascending to God).
The poet then abandons the botanical similitude and compares Christ
to the penetrative point of a needle that can be stayed by 'non
armure' or 'none heiȝ walles'. Undoubtly, the armour refers to the
Roman soldiers guarding the tomb of Christ. The 'heiȝ walles'
perhaps refers to the emprisoning fortress of hell whose defences
Christ is to pierce in his redemption of souls. The 'high-walls' and
their connection with hell may be a memory of Deuteronomy 3.5:
'Cunctae urbes erant munitae muris altissimus...', describing the
cities of the Kingdom of Og in Bashan. Augustine in his commentary
on Psalm 135.20 identifies Og with the devil. Compare the poor and
the meek thrusting their way into the palace of heaven in Passus X:

Souteres and sheperdes, suche lewed iottes,
percen with a pater-noster þe paleys of heuene...

(X. 460-1)
[fol. 43b]

The contrastive, antithetical force of the images shows a certain
patterning: heavy/light, rooting/leaves, sharpness/impenetrableness,
terrestial/infernal; an alternation of downward/upward movements,
flickering in quick succession, suggesting the play of energy, a release
of power. The actual passion has been ellipsed as a sequence and as
soon as the poet has finished his first mixed similitude, he then alters
the imagery and relaxes the rhythm of his lines, expanding more
slowly and less urgently into a moralization of the previous imagistic
compound, dwelling on the main points of doctrine: love, mercy, and
pity. At the same time, Langland has not abandoned word-play or
paradox. One notices that the technical term for payment for pardon
(to the Crown) *amercement* has been skilfully transposed into the noun
merciment. The 'fine' Christ imposes (by justice) is not a fine but
perfect 'mercy'. This, again, looks forward to Langland's deliberate
use of the Anselmian compound *Deus-homo* in Passus XI. The line
(162): 'And in the herte þere is þe heuede and þe heiȝ welle' must
have pleased the poet in its emphatic contrasting of head and heart (in

different senses) and the counterbalancing echo of 'heiȝ welle' (of
mercy and love) with the 'heiȝ walles' (156) of the loveless confines of
Lucifer's prison. Gradually, by the end of the passage we reach the
Passion, but only briefly touched on. Here, too, Christ's dual nature
is emphatically stressed. As Professor Bennett remarks: 'The Dual
Nature is the mainspring of much of Langland's theology'.

> Here myȝtow see ensaumples in hymselue one,
> That he was miȝtful and meke and mercy gan graunte
> To hem þat hongen him an heiȝ and his herte þirled.
>
> (I. 170-173).

The power which Christ retains even on the Cross matches, and is the
source of, that 'myȝte' which begins in the human heart through
'kynde knowynge' mentioned but a few lines before:

> For in kynde knowynge in herte þere a myȝte bigynneth
>
> (I. 163)

In the programme of the poem, in its concern with social institutions, satiric commentary and the progress of the Lady Meed, the
poet returns hardly at all to the figure of Christ or even to oblique
images of, or allusions to, the second person of the Trinity. Christ, in
effect, disappears from the poem, except to be invoked in oaths,
seldom meant and often idly spoken, a mere echo of his reality. Christ
reappears suddenly and with the same emphasis on mercy and pity,
an emphasis which connects directly with the passage just discussed.
He appears obliquely, addressed by the robber Robert in the transitional passage in Passus V. 469 ff. It is the crucified Christ (still on the
cross) who is addressed (however dishonestly) by the thief. The mood
of penitence interlocks this passage with the actual prayer of Repen-
tance, and the image of the crucified Christ anticipates and interlocks
with the triumphal, Easter-oriented lyrical presentation of the Passion
in all its nervous rhythm and insistent Latin biblical and liturgical
reminiscence.

The artistic method of Langland in creating this lyrical tableau (V.
488-519) is mainly characterized by accumulation, intercalation and
association. The associative texture is especially pronounced in the
liturgical use of Latin texts and their Easter application. The Latin
lines themselves have verbal features which assist the alliterative pulse
of the English words: emphatic repeating of rhetorical and grammatical patterns, strong repetitions of case endings (especially the

accusative singular). Professor Bennett's notes should be consulted in order to trace the intricate relation of the liturgical use of Vulgate text with the dominant Easter and resurrection mood. But the real triumph of composition lies in the English poetry and its reintroduction of image-clusters which the reader will recall from the passage in Passus I. 150 ff. The cluster of feeding/blood/fulness/light/leaping/ ransoming of souls is unmistakable in both passages, though the rhythm in Passus V is more intense and the culminating and unique image of the 'blowing' by Christ's breath of the souls into bliss (which in turn generates the associated image of 'the horn of Hope' and the blowing of *Beata quorum remisse sunt iniquitates*) give us a new musical climax formed of an antiphonal structure: the souls in heaven singing in unison, answered by the massed voices of humanity calling out for permission to seek out Truth. There seems a certain pictorial arrangement of Christ and the Blessed Virgin surrounded above and below by massed saints and human crowds. No one certain religious iconography is being drawn on. Further, the chivalric cluster of images is picked up (508), Christ's dual nature and themes of mercy and pity given their central resonance. Word-play of a traditional nature (*sone/sunne*) is reinforced by extensions of traditional ideas: *sute/sute*, repeated twice in the collocation 'in oure sute' in lines 495 and 504. Phraseological balance is restored to; *no sorowe/þe sorowe*; *synful Marie/seynte Marie*. Certain consonantal groups predominate in alliteration, notably, *s, m* and the group *b(1)* which yields: *blent/blewe/blissed/blisse/blew/Beati*.

The overall effect of this poetic creation is of associative immersion. The reader is bathed in sounds and images, as if he were sitting in church during a service, surrounded by stone images, stained glass and sung liturgy. There is none of the evocative verbal recreation of a liturgical style of the kind which we now trace to the aureation of the Bury monk. Yet Langland at an earlier date supplies in these intense, complexly associative renderings of the Incarnation and the Passion, the synaesthetic effect of the essential poetry of experienced ritual, of a fused religious-artistic interplay of moral awareness, not in the least traditionally or aesthetically 'beautiful' or abstracting. One remembers Ruskin's remark on the function of association:

> For I believe that mere pleasure and pain have less associative power than duty performed or omitted, and that the great use of the Associative faculty is not to add beauty to material things, but to add force to the Conscience.[10]

After the identification of Christ with Dowel in the *conclusio* of Passus VII (195-200), the person of Christ, oblique and direct, drops out of the poem. The predominant pressures seem to be personal, psychological and satiric. In all the rambling instruction of Wit in Passus IX there is but one firm reference to Christ, and that is plainly an aside, lost in the growing antimatrimonial ruminations. The whole passage is 'rationalized' in the C-Text and the note of bitterness and the sardonic tone in the reference to Christ have been removed. In the B-Text, the aside (line 159): 'I am *via et veritas*, seith Cryst, 'I may auance alle' sees the words of John 14.6 lifted out of context and grafted on to words which do not belong to the context. 'Auance' is a strange verb, the general editorial persuasion is that it means 'aid' or 'assist', but it is difficult to find the place where Christ says these words. The oblique reference to John 14.6 perhaps requires to be treated with circumspection. 'Circumspection' is probably the right watch-word for one's approach to much of the confused and disorganized episodes thrown up by the introspective environment of the self-searching excursions which unfold from Passus VIII up to Passus XVI. The main emphases of these Passus seem to lie in the personifying edification of the poet's mental powers or functions of the mind: Wit and Thought in Passus VIII, the House of Anima in Passus IX, Wit, Study and Learning in Passus X, Fortune and Nature in XI, Imaginatyf in XII, Conscience in XIII and XIV, Anima in XV. Passus X (where Christ again appears somewhat marginally) though it possesses a simple plot as a series of interviews, is profoundly digressive and diffuse in argument. The overall effect of X is accumulatively depressing. It lacks a programmatic direction as well as a lively sense of reality. The author himself exclaims at one point: 'This is a longe lessoun ... and litel am I the wyser' (372). The reader is tempted to add his own 'amen'. In the dreamer's attempt to identify Dowel and Dobet, the argument strays away from the putative function of *dominus* and 'kniȝthode' into salvation and heaven. At this point Scripture brings Christ into his argument concerning the salvation of souls (lines 353 ff.):

> Ac Crysten men with-oute more may nouȝt come to heuene,
> For þat Cryst for Cristenmen deyde, and confirmed þe lawe,
> Þat who-so wolde and wylneth with Criste to aryse,
> > *Si cum Christo surrexistis etc.*
> He shulde louvye and leue and þe lawe fulfille.

[fol. 42a]

Although there is nothing surprising in the argument and the ex-emplification ordinary enough, yet it is Christ crucified who supplies the reference. Similarly, as the dreamer turns the arguments over and over he comes back to the same Christ crucified who had been prayed to by Robert the robber in Passus V:

> On Gode Fridaye I fynde a feloun was ysaued,
> Þat had lyued al his lyf with lesynges and with thefte;
> And for he biknewe on þe crosse and to Cryste scrof hym,
> He was sonnere saued þa[n] seynt Iohan Baptiste,
> And or Adam or Yseye, or eny of þe prophetes,
> Þat hadde yleine with Lucyfer many longe ȝeres.

> > (X. 414 ff.)
> > [fol. 43a]

The whole Passus runs with a groundswell of anti-intellectualism which carries over into Passus XI. Again, in this Passus the same emphasis on the crucified Christ and his redemptive power is repeated in the Emperor Trajan's long and sometimes eloquent exposition—beginning with the anti-intellectual exclamation 'ȝee, baw for bokes!' (135). Trajan's exposition of the figure of Christ is significant in its Anselmian emphasis and interesting in that it develops a more historical aspect of the life of Christ than we have seen hitherto in the poem, mainly by way of the gospel of St John and Christ's explicit connection with poverty and humility. It also provides an opportunity to concentrate on 'works' and activity:

> Why I moue þis matere is moste for þe pore,
> For in her lyknesse owre lorde ofte hath ben yknowe.
> Witnesse in þe Paske-wyke whan he ȝede to *Emaus*;
> Cleophas ne knewe hym nauȝte, þat he *Cryste* were,
> For his pore paraille and pylgrymes wedes,
> Tyl he blessed and brak þe bred þat þei eten,
> So bi his werkes þei wisten þat he was *Iesus*;

> > (XI. 224-231)
> > [fol. 46b]

The sudden appearance of Imaginatyf in the dying moments of Passus XI. 401 ff. and his defence of Learning and *Ratio* brings the anti-intellectual colouring of the general argument to an end. It is no great surprise, therefore, that when Imaginatyf comes to his imagining of Christ in Passus XII, one finds reintroduced Langland's own formerly stated appreciation of scholarship and love. The episode is taken again from the gospel of St John (the mainspring of the last image in Passus XI). Here (lines 72 ff.) the proof that Christ's love is the 'root' of learning is taken from John 8.3-9, embellished by Augustine's observations on this passage in the *Expositio in Evangelium Joannis* (*cap.* 33 on John 8.6 ff.). The whole of Imaginatyf's discourse down to line 140 contains reminiscences of the Augustinian exposition. The association with 'goddes body' in lines 88 and 92 seems to reflect Augustine's contrast between the Old and New Testament (Exodus 31 and John):

> Digito enim Dei lex scripta est, Dei propter duros in lapide scripta est. Nunc iam dominus in terra scribebat, quia fructum quaerebat.

The emphasis naturally falls on self-knowledge and innate understanding. Christ's words in John 8 focus upon the individual conscience (as the Pharisees reminded Him later when they returned). But the natural development of Imaginatyf's arguments is loose and chiefly associative; by various windings he finally comes to the Nativity (lines 142 ff.) which is also given a moralization which contrasts the world, the rich, and the powerful (and the friars!) with the learned and the humble. After more windings we arrive back at the crucifixion, Good Friday and the saved thief (lines 201-209). The effect of Passus XII is one of the diffuseness and lack of proper poetic concentration. We even meander back over the Trajan material again—material which is still fresh in the reader's memory. Trajan's own exposition is far more concentrated in poetic emphasis; the recapitulation only weakens the original memorableness.

Christ again disappears from the poem until we are well into the quagmire of Passus XV when, at last, Anima acknowledges the deep and necessary connection between Piers Plowman and Christ in answer to the question of what is charity. The poet here departs from his earlier methods of presenting Christ, (that is, by tending to use an image or image-cluster from which discursive elaboration or commentary-type expositions are then extended). The method pursued in Passus XV is fundamentally discursive and oratorical. The lack of imagistic concentricity corresponds with, and provides an equivalent for, the multiform, variousness of the appearances on earth of the figure of Christ/Piers/Charity. Langland has recourse to 'exemplary figures' and the main poetic texture consists in the open use of rhetorical figures of speech, especially *repetitio* ('ne ... ne'), *parison* ('I haue seen ... in + adj./in + sb.), *exclamatio* and *anaphora* ('Ac ... ac'). The effect is one of rhetorical spaciousness (compare the extension of syntactical units) and a certain modest and measured eloquence which reminds one of the traditional 'ornatus' of the rhetoricians. The problem which arises from the poet's adoption of this technique is that the oratorical address goes on for far too long and soon the original rhetorical orientation and shapeliness is lost in continuous elaboration. I quote the first twenty-three lines of the speech:

> Þerefore by coloure ne by clergye knowe shaltow hym neuere,
> Noyther þorw wordes ne werkes but þorw wille one.
> And þat knoweth no clerke, ne creature in erthe,
> But Piers þe Plowman—*Petrus id est Christus.*
> For he ne is nouȝte in lolleres, ne in lande-leperes hermytes,
> Ne at ancres, þere a box hangeth alle suche þei faiten.
> Fy on faitoures and *in fautores suos!*
> For charyte is goddis champioun and as a good chylde hende,
> And þe meryst of mouth at mete where he sitteth.
> Þe loue þat lith in his herte maketh hym lyȝte of speche
> And is compenable and confortatyf, as Cryst bit hymselue,
>   *Nolite fieri sicut ypocrite, tristes etc.*
> For I haue seyn hym in sylke and somme tyme in russet,
> Bothe in grey and in grys and in gulte herneys,
> And as gladlich he it gaf to gomes þat it neded.
> Edmonde and Edwarde eyther were kynges,
> And seyntes ysette tyl charite hem folwed.
> I haue seyne Charite also syngen and reden,
> Ryden and rennen in ragged wedes,
> Ac biddyng as beggeres bihelde I hym neuere.
> Ac in riche robes rathest he walketh,
> Ycalled and ycrimiled and his crowne shaue;

[fols. 64b-65a]

The floridly imagined Tree of Patience in Passus XVI (already discussed) has the effect of concentrating the narrative line of the poem, turning the diffuse, inward self-debate back into the waking world with a change in symbolic time and geography. In the unfolding of Passus XVI and XVII the dreamer is turned 'to Jhersalemward' and historically placed in a re-experiencing of the time of the Old Testament as it connects with, and anticipates the foundation of the New Testament through Christ's life. The fulfilment of prophetic passages is made repeated use of. Abraham's words at the end of Passus XVI fully anticipate the events of Passus XVIII. Similarly, the mixt allegorical mode of Passus XVII pursues and extends the same repetitious, anticipatory techniques: exampla, schematic allegories and moralizations serve to attempt to direct the poet's mind towards the culminating experience of Passus XVIII. Aspects of Christ can be seen diffused throughout XVI and XVII, but whether oblique or direct, there is no sustained poetic concentration on arresting Christocentric material. The set-piece of Passus XVII lies in the exposition of the Trinity using the schematic *allegoria* of the human hand (lines 138-203), closely followed by another schematic exposition in the imagery of the torch or taper (204 ff.). The torch or taper analogue was probably suggested by St Augustine, *De Trinitate* (*lib.* VI) from the images of brightness and fire. The origin of the Trinity as fist, palm and finger is almost certainly original, compounded of various applications of the hand to persons of the Trinity separately: the 'mundum pugillo continens' of the breviary hymn (as applied to God the Father) suggested by Isaiah 40, 12 (as Skeat observed), supplemented by the common application of *filius* as 'Manus Dei est' 'Isidore, *Etymologiae* VII) and the Holy Spirit as 'Digitus Dei' (Isidore, *ibid.*). The anatomy has been partially reassigned and the whole, tedious schematic analogousness further elaborated and extended. The second *schema*, that of torch or taper, generates more interesting poetic language:

> ... as glowande gledes gladieth nouȝte þis werkmen
> Þat worchen and waken in wynteres niȝtes ...

(217-8)

Melteth in a mynut-while to myst and to watre ...[12]

(228)

but these set-pieces themselves melt away into more unfocused and unconcentrated narrative excursus. The final distinctions concerning sinfulness as enumerated by the Samaritan seem oddly weakening of the proper use of anticipatory narrative devices. One is constantly aware of wishing that the glancing reference to Christ were better organized and less vitiated by the unsustained thematic pressures—more like a water-garden, less like a swamp.

When we finally reach Passus XVIII a very few lines convince us that at last Langland has left the marshy low 'mid-lenten' country, desisted from skirmishing and retreating, mustered his poetic forces to make a fight of it on higher ground with a clear field of fire to the enemy. Indirection and intercalation of narrative method is retained but the poetic concentration and concrete sense of reality we found in Passus I and Passus V have returned. Moreover, we realize from the very start that the poet means to treat this Christocentric tableau in a full sequential pattern. It will command the full weight of his poetic attention.

The poetic method pursued in Passus XVIII closely resembles the technique evolved for Passus V: image-clustering, narrative inter-calation, liturgical resonance (with Easter association), condensed and original use of lyrical language. The narrative extendedness of Passus XVIII shows the original pattern of V expanded and therefore altered. The technique may be compared in sewing to a chain-stitch: where each forward movement of the narrative generates a space, an ellipsis, which backward loops of the narrative fill in and in turn throw the narrative line forward again. But the thread of this nar-rative chain-stitch is also made up of different colours, of different dimensions of the Christ story. Time is used kaleidoscopically, figures are compounded of realism, moralization, allegorization and figurative extension; gospel-based narrative is blended with contem-porary symbolism and reference; dramatic and realistic sequence in-terrupted by prophetic or symbolic material imported from the apocryphal gospel of Nicodemus or that great bore the *Legenda Aurea*. Intercalation of episodes and dimensions is a constant feature of the entire Passus and Langland manages this whole complex narrative structure in a masterly fashion. It seems to me that he only strikes two discordant notes: the long outburst of Faith against the Jews and the anathema pronounced (lines 92-109). This seems not to add significantly to the tension-energy of the sequence. Similarly, I find unnecessary the intervention of 'Book' (*Sanctas Scripturas*[13]) as 'witness' to the end of the Four Daughters of God's discussion prior to the Harrowing of Hell sequence (lines 228-257). His tedious renar-rating seems also to relax the narrative tension in exactly the wrong place. Truth interrupts his witness, politely bidding the whole com-pany to be quiet ('suffre we') at line 228—Truth had used this same command earlier at line 167.

Whilst the effect of similar poetic invention in Passus V can be compared to the experience of enacted ritual, a lyrical immersion of the reader in images and sound, the extended 'chain-stitch' narrative technique of Passus XVIII produces a new effect on the reader. With the prolongation of the narrative and the more complex intercalation of dimensions, there is created a pattern of alterations and substitutions in which complex porportions are constantly being brought into being in such a way that the reader undergoes a sustained programme of active and heightened awareness. Perhaps it would be fair to say that the reader experiences a sustained period of aesthetic excitement akin to participating in a celebratory mood in which several activities are combining and recombining to create an effect of prolonged stimulation or dramatic excitement—if we may take the final tableau of the Passus as an analogy, a celebration in which instrumental music, song and dance are joined (lines 421-424) into a unified expression of joy. These final lines bring the formal power of the whole Passus into a summarizing representation of the actual process which Langland has been creating throughout the whole development of the narrative sequence. This festival of spiritual celebration and the reader's participation in the spirit of release requires a partially musical analogy, though Langland's poetic invention in its complex formal evolution would find no exact analogue or counterpart in the real medieval world of experience, one feels. The poetic recreation goes beyond medieval inventions in music, dance or the dramatic. Prudentius in his poem *Apotheosis* attempts a kind of rhetorical movement of panegyrical celebration which endeavours to create much the same sense of excitement—and he also calls upon images of music and song to summon the moment into being:

Quidquid in ære cavo reboans turba curva remugit,
Quidquid ab arcano vomit ingens spiritus haustu,
Quidquid casta chelys, quidquid testudo resultat,
Organa disparibus calamis quod consona miscent,
Æmula pastorum quod reddunt vocibus antra,
Christum concelebrat, Christum sonat;

(384-391)

All the loud music which rings on the curved trumpet's
hollow metal, all that the vast deep-drawn breath
abundantly pours forth, all the resounding notes
of holy harp and lyre, all the mingled harmony of
tuned and unequal organ-pipes, all the songs which
grottos in rivalry re-echo to the shepherds'
voices, all proclaim Christ and sound Christ's name.

The medium open to Prudentius is that which he knew and admired: all the resources of the figures and tropes of classical rhetoric and the rhythms and word-order of his beloved Virgil. Langland is less restricted: his methods are composite in origin, most of them non-literary. His final triumph of narrative excitement and amalgamization is totally original. This originality is made possible by several factors. First, by continually trying out various aspects of Christ's life and ministry using a variety of expressive techniques in the Passus from VIII to XVII, Langland provided himself with the accumulated evidence of what could be discarded in terms of subject and technical handling. By this means, for example, the florid grotesque of imposed allegories of Passus XVI could be ruled out, as well as having the emotion which called it into being indulged, and so moderated. When all the subjects, aspects of themes and techniques had been tried, I believe Langland turned back to the great Christocentric passage in Passus V and borrowed from himself: evolving the new 'chain-stitch' narrative method from his own earlier, poetic invention.

Although the effect on the reader of Passus V. 486-519 is different, yet the intercalation of thematic emphasis with progressive, direct narrative is present in a less well-developed form. The following paradigm may be abstracted from the Passus V unit:

A: *orison*: theme: Christ's suffering for mankind

(489-91)

B: Latin: *exclamatio* (reflective)

C: narrative (oblique): incarnation

B: Latin: *expolitio* of incarnation and theme A.

C: narrative (direct); crucifixion.

B: Latin: Ephesians 4.8. anticipates narrative (harrowing of Hell).

C: narrative (direct): crucifixion, the feeding of apostles and souls in hell.

B: Latin: Isaiah 9.2. Christ as light.

C: narrative (direct): harrowing of Hell, blinding of Satan.

C: narrative (direct): re-incarnation and appearance to Mary Magdalen.

(indirect): leading back into theme A of prayer.

B: Latin: Luke 5.32: development of theme A.

D: Summary and chivalry image.

B: Latin: orchestrates A and summary.

A: *orison*.

E: *conclusio*: musical images and Easter associations.

Passus XVIII sees this type of poetic procedure given a much more complex and extended treatment. The narrative is made more sequential and detailed realism added. The intercalation is given several dimensions of planes of reference. The role of Latin quotation is changed: far less use is made of whole single line juxtaposition (until we reach the conclusion). Langland uses phrases more freely mixed with the ME. In terms of sheer amount, there is far more ME to Latin. In a way, the principle of multidimensional intercalation in XVIII has taken over the function of Latin texts as used in Passus V. The popular texts which lie behind the harrowing of hell are fully drawn on. The *conclusio* of V (which forms the major climax) is retained as *conclusio* in XVIII but the climax (and central imagistic emphasis) is shifted to the dramatic action of the harrowing as witnessed by Truth. The central imagistic emphasis in the light-bearing imagery of Isaiah 9.2 and the blinding of Satan is given a complex, emphatic pattern in *repetitio* or *ploce*. The germ of all this is present in Passus V. 489-519, but the technical advance in XVIII is startling. Like Passus V, the alliterative formulation creates key-words and key repetitions, and these key-words in repeated associations create dominant image-clusters. In Dunbar's *Done is a Battel on the Dragon Black* there is a deliberate use of *partitio* and *repetitio* as plot-structure with a repeated use of phonetic symbolism: the heavy, repeated trochaic alliterative pattern symbolizes both the 'knell of mercy' (line 29)—the Easter bells—and what the ringing actually symbolizes, the breaking down of the gates of hell: 'The ʒetis of hell are brokin with a crack' (line 3). The idea of this phonetic connection is not restricted to Dunbar but may be found amongst the Anglo-Latin poets. There is a particularly moving use of this rhythmic association in the poetry of John of Howden, in the *Quinquagenta Canta*:

> Aspis et leo pavimentis equantur
> proprio perimitur ydra squalore;
> imo reconditi thesauri monstrantur,
> Et mors invehitur in mortis auctore.

Something like the intensity of Dunbar's patterning may be found in Langland. In Passus XVIII, at the precise moment when Christ 'emisit spiritum', the death of 'god-man', the poet invents a memorable line, full of quietude and acquiescence, reflecting almost the calmness of sleep:

þe lorde of lyf and of liȝte þo leyed his eyen togideres

(59)
[fol. 77a]

'eyen' is a shortened, substitute expression for 'eye-lid' and a passage in Marjorie Kempe makes clear the association of the expression 'leyed togideres' with sleep: 'His ey-leyds went a lytil to-gedyr with a maner of slepe'[14]. Langland's single line (59) establishes a cluster of key-words and images: *lord/lyf/liȝte/eyen*. The very next moment of climax and dramatic emphasis, when Longeus's sight is instantly restored as a consequence of the piercing of Christ's side and heart, exploits one of the terms of the same cluster:

Þe blode spronge down by þe spere and vnspered þe kniȝtes eyen
(86)
[fol. 77b]

the actions of 'leyed his eyen togederes' and 'vnspered þe kniȝtes eyen' are dramatically and antithetically contrasted and the *traductio* between 'spere' and 'vnspered' assists in adding another key-word to the original clust of *lord/lyf/liȝte/eyen*, 'vnspere' to unbar, 'unlock'. We are being gently directed towards the central image of the 'unlocking' of hell's gates. The function of the eye is, of course, to 'look' and that verb, too, will soon join the image-cluster. The central pattern is gradually exfoliated as the narrative develops. The consistency of emphasis and clustering is remarkable:

124:    And which a liȝte and a leme lay befor helle
[fol. 77b]
137:    Þe while þis liȝte and þis leme shal Lucyfer ablende
[fol. 78a]
187:    Leuestow þat ȝonde liȝte vnlouke myȝte helle
[78b]
243:    And lo how þe sonne gan louke her liȝte in her-self
[79a]
255:    And al þe iuwen ioye vnioignen and vnlouken
[79b]
259:    How a spirit speketh to helle and bit vnspere þe ȝatis
[79b]
260:    A voice loude in þat liȝte to Lucifer cryeth
'Prynces of þis place vnpynneth and vnlouketh'
[79b]

269:     Þat such a lorde and a lyȝte shulde lede hem alle hennes

[79b]

313:     Efte þe liȝte bad vnlouke and Lucifer answered

[80a]

323:     Lucyfer loke ne myȝte so lyȝte hym ableynte

[80a]

381:     Lawe wolde, he ȝeue hym lyf, if he loked on hym

[80b]

383:     And ȝif lawe wil I-loke on hem, it lithe in my grace

[81a]

403:     They dorste nouȝte loke on owre lorde, þe boldest of hem
         alle

[81a]

This clustering generates a secondary row of key-words, notably, *Loue/lauȝhynge/loude*. Even taken out of context each of these key lines conveys nearly the whole of its subject and theme, and conveys with lyric economy the crucial sense of *release*, of newly created freedom, The source of that freedom and the impotence of the *di inferni* to resist. The secondary key-words provide the final note of universal rejoicing:

And thanne luted Loue in a loude note,
Ecce quam bonum et quam iocundum etc.

[fol. 81b]

The opening line of Vulgate Psalm 132 reminds us of unity: 'habitare fratres in *vnum*'. The connection with love is stressed in Augustine's commentary on this verse: 'Tam dulcis et quam dulcis est *charitas*, quae fuit fratres habitare in vnum.' He also comments: 'Iste versus fuit tuba ipsorum, sonuit per orbem terrarum ...'. What is less obvious is Langland's unique use of the noun 'lute' as a verb, recorded nowhere else in ME. The attributive vb. is in parallel with 'tromped' in the line before and so naturally stresses the instrumental accompaniment. Professor Burrow reminds us that in the Chester and Towneley Plays, the Matins hymn 'Te Deum laudamus' ('tromped' by Truth) is associated with the harrowing of hell. It should also be remembered that of all the Matins Hymns it is sung last, and so serves to introduce the office of Lauds, with its central insistence on light, Christ the 'cock', the bringer of light, the triumph of day over night which lies at the heart of this Passus, as this imagery dominates all the hymns of Lauds.[15] It should also be noted that this final, triumphal Psalm 132 is associated by Augustine with the Crucifixion and the Ascension, and the Psalm is in regular use as a morning prayer. Langland wonderfully connects this triumph of light with the actual moment of celebration:

> Tyl þe daye dawed þis damaiseles daunced
> That men ronged to þe resurexion and riȝt with that I waked ...
>
> [fol. 81b]

The dance referred to here is a variation on the 'Dance of the Blessed', a *topos* not unknown to visual artists or the poets.[16] The *topos* originates in the Psalm text 149.3: 'Laudent nomen eius in choro'. Augustine in his enarration remarks: 'Chorus Christi iam totus mundus est. Chorus Christi ab Oriente in Occidentem consonat.' Here Langland transfers the dancing to the Four Daughters of God, using the text of Psalm 67.25. In some manuscripts of the C-Text the 'damoyselles caroled'. Peace had announced this celebration earlier in lines 178-9:

> Moyses and many mo merry shal haue,
> And I shal daunce þer-to, do þow so, sustre,
> For Ihesus iusted wel, ioye bygynneth dawe;
>
> [fol. 78b]

Line 6 of Vulgate Psalm 29 is quoted:

> *Ad vesperum demorabitur fletus, et ad matutinum leticia.*

Augustine comments on this dawn and rejoicing: 'Nam ideo et dominus Iesus Christus in matutino surrexit de sepulchro ...'.

After the creative energy, the lyrical and narrative excitement of Passus XVIII, Passus XIX, dreamed in a separate dream and after the act of poetic composition ('wrote what I had dreamed'), seems almost too calm and anticlimactic. It seems to provide for the poet-dreamer a form of settled *expositio* on the text of Passus XVIII. It is delivered by Conscience in answer to repeated questions from the author, who, after all the preparatory expositions of the pre-XVIII material, and the crowning Passus itself, knows only too well the answers. Actually, this *expositio* (really a collection of explanatory analogies, a re-capitulation of gospel material, a little biblical exegesis and schematic allegory) exists for the benefit of the reader. It is the equivalent of 'reinforcement learning' and Conscience has immediate recourse to the kinds of medieval analogies and imagery which bring far-off biblical material well within the scope of fourteenth-century demonstration and instruction. Hence the armorial images, the use of feudal relationships, functions and duties (26-64), the gospel-based Nativity followed by the foreshortened vita (65 ff., identified with Dowel), the miracles (an increase in power, identified with Dobet), the sudden condensed arrest, trial, death and all the subsequent events thereafter leading up to the establishing of the apostolic ministry (identified with Dobest); where the name of Piers is transferred from Christ to Peter. This summary lesson ends at line 193. Christ evaporates from the exposition and the narrative develops a new, instructional direction. For the first time we hear the ominous name Antichrist, and the church expressed as the 'house of Unity'.

Awake and indigent in the last Passus, XX, the author returns to a realistic experience of the world and society which recalls the full contemporanity of the opening of the poem in the Prologue. Before he falls to dream again (line 50), Need, stark necessity, introduces the poet-figure to the last sustained image of Christ we are to receive in the world of the poem—the poor, needy Christ we glimpsed long ago in Trajan's earnest speech in Passus XI. This time the image and text is not based on the gospel of John but on Matthew 8.20, when an unnamed scribe attached himself to Christ and promised to follow him, and Christ answered with the bleak words: 'Vulpes foveas habent, et volucres cæli nidos: Filius autem hominis non habet ubi caput reclinet'; 'The foxes have holes, and the birds of the air have nests; but the Son of Man hath not where to lay his head.' In Passus XX the occasion is changed: the words are now spoken from the cross (as if part of the Reproaches of Good Friday) but with the message utterly changed: 'And [I] suffre ful sowre that shal to Ioye tourne.' The emphatic return to the crucified Christ—who now utters no reproaches but makes a joyful promise—is deliberate and characteristic. The last words spoken from the cross were originally those of Christ in John 16.20, the promises made to the disciples, looking forward to the resurrection and the Ascension: 'vos autem contristabimini sed tristitia vestra veretur in gaudium'. The transfer of the words of Matthew 8 and John 16 to Christ on the cross seem to be original. Need's message provides the author-figure with a draught of pure resignation. As the hectic events of his final dream unfold, 'this scribe' will have need of every bit of resignation—or to use Trajan's word, 'pacience'. His contemporary world in dream dissolves into disunity and discord. That same Petrus to whom the name of Piers has passed also testifies in his second general letter (2 Peter 3.15.) that 'the long-suffering of Christ *is* salvation'[17]: 'Et Domini nostri longanimitatem, salutem arbitremini ...'). The definition of Piers Plowman by Anima (XV. 205-262) should be remembered, especially lines 255-262. Perhaps we should also be reminded that the word-play of Passus XV. 148: 'I haue lyued in londe ... my name is longe Wille', not only hints at the surname which we now accept as that of the poet, but also hints at an English equivalant for the Latin noun *longanimitas*, *longanima*, 'long-sufference'.[18]

CHAPTER SIX

Psychological Vocabulary and Images of Mental Processes

He o'er festooning every interval,
As the adventurous spider, making light
Of distance shoots her threads from depth to height,
From barbican to battlement: so flung
Fantasies forth and in their centre swung
Our architect—

Robert Browning, *Sordello*, book I

The aim of this inquiry is not to attempt to reconstruct from the evidence of the poem or the poet's learning representation of Langland's 'mind' but to examine the lexical resources of the writer when they are employed to describe or embody mental activities, whether those of remembering, acts of reasoning, or irrational mental activities such as fear or anxiety. Beyond these lexical resources, we should also examine more extended poetic constructs, for the sake of brevity called 'images' of processes or activities which belong to the area of mental behaviour. Because of the non-literary nature of most of the sources of Langland's creative activity and the 'unmedieval' characteristics of his handling of allegory and narrative it is important to attempt to evaluate how typical or atypical was the poet's account of mental process itself, whether we can eventually attribute these processes to the poet's mind or other minds fashioned in the course of literary characterization or personification. Further, if Dr Mill's theory is correct (as I believe it to be), that the perceptions of the poet as author and the dreamer as narrator or narrator-character are identical or nearly identical—that the reflective experience shows no significant distance and mental separateness or significant mediation, then our investigation into the poetic representation of acts of cognition should confirm or deny that theory that it is not possible to distinguish between 'thought' and 'expression' and that Langland 'is faced with the problem of talking about an ideal infinite with the outlook and language of a corrupt finite'.[1]

Of course, the question of 'typicalness' is hedged round with difficulties and uncertainties. Comparison with substantial contemporary poets writing during the years 1373-1390 cannot be avoided. Gower and Chaucer must present themselves for relative judgment and estimation. One wishes that some work, some substantial work, could be traced to the other London poet of the time, Ralph Strode.[2] At the same time we must allow ourselves to ask how far were poets writing about processes which could be described as 'mental' influenced by philosophical theorizing and what could be called mental philosophy or psychological activity? Here the area for investigation becomes almost impossible to cover. So much of the philosophical writing remains unedited and unprinted, much less evaluated or read by medievalists. How many works were merely commentaries, how many original treatises, how many *Questiones* were substantially original in thought? The potential list of authors writing in Latin is large, unexpectedly large. Some authors are well-known, the majority obscure. Augustine and Avicenna we recognize and may have read, but who can have read the Englishman John Baconthorpe's commentaries on Aristotle's *De Anima*, *De Somno et Vigilia* and the *De Potentiis Animæ*? He appears to have been a contemporary of Walter Burley (*fl.* 1305-44), or Adam Buckfield[3] of an earlier period (*fl.* 1250), Canon of Lincoln, who probably wrote commentaries to the *De Sensu et Sensato*, *De Somno et Vigilia* and *De Anima*. The most active of the philosophical schools in England, the 'Merton School' at Oxford (first half of the fourteenth century) appears to have been chiefly interested in natural philosophy, mathematics and physics.[4] Yet Walter Burley (who is sometimes numbered among the Mertonists) wrote much on mental philosophy, much that indicates a thoroughly Aristotelian training and interest. On 'Aristotelian' texts we have commentaries on the *De Anima*, *De Sensu et Sensato*, *De Somno et Vigilia*, *De Sensibus*, *De Memoria*, and in Oriel College MS. 12 something called *Tractatus de quinque sensibus*. Weisheipl also gives us *Questiones super libros de Anima* (Cambridge, Caius Coll. MS. 668) and a *Tractatus de Potentiis Animæ* (Oxford, Magdalen Coll. MS. 145). The list of possible philosophical authors is huge and the following footnote may prove of some use to those willing to read the vast amount of manuscript material.[5]

What sort of theories, roughly, would a medieval poet be exposed to, say, if he were in the mood to be influenced by scientific writings on the operations of the mind or soul? From my reading experience, I believe he would find two major types of theory and four main channels of written transmission. The two major theories may be divided between (1) the patristic, theologically influenced accounts of the soul which descend undoubtedly from Augustine's writings, chiefly the *Anima et Spiritu* and the *De Quantitate Animæ*; and (2) the Aristotelian writings and their accompanying commentaries and *questiones*, namely, the *De Anima, De Memoria et Reminiscentia, De Somno et Vigilia*. The four main channels of transmission were: Augustine and Aristotle directly or indirectly, together with Cassiodorus's *De Anima* (strongly influenced by Augustinian notions) and the carrier force of the encyclopaedists, especially Isidore and Vincent of Beauvais. Of the last, Vincent provides evidence for any and nearly every view you might wish to find—the resumés of Aristotle are particularly good. The *Specula* are so organized that 'topics' collect opposing arguments and evidence, including references. Isidore's account (*Etymologiæ* XI. i. 'De homine et partibus eius') is manifestly influenced by Cassiodorus (*De Anima*, cap. 3) and Augustine, *De Spiritu et Anima* I. 34, and so is Augustinian in emphasis. Augustinian and Aristotelian notions on the operations of the soul and the function of mind are completely distinct. In the Augustinian account there is a complete separation between soul and corporality which makes a systematic and detailed study of sense perception, the operation of memory, the functions of cognition, the involvement of emotions, nearly pointless. The origin of this 'purity' of the operation of rational activity can be found in Plato (*Theaetetus* 184B-186E). The spirit's proper function is rational thought which apprehends incorporeal and invisible reality. Reason is best exercised when the human spirit separates itself from fleshly interferences so as to think by itself. The reality it contemplates and recognizes has its existence guaranteed by the operation of the Divine Mind, author both of external reality and the rational activity which apprehends this 'reality'. All this is enshrined in Augustine's *De Spiritu et Anima* I.32. Although splendid patristic bricks and mortar, it makes, alas, for a primitive and uninteresting form of mental philosophy. It can assign abstractly 'functions' to mind and senses in a paradigmatic language but leaves any detailed description of 'function' and cooperation with sense experience undeveloped and unexpressed. The real business of the soul and its pure rationality is to know God—like recollecting or recognizing Forms in Plato. All that is troublesome and 'deceptive' in Plato and Augustine is interesting to

Aristotle, for here there is no separation between soul or mind and corporality. There is an intrinsic connection: every mental occurrence, including thoughts, images etc., is, amongst other things, a physiological entity (*De Anima* 403a 25-9b). Mental occurrences are common to the soul and the body; they do not belong to separate substances.

But did any of the three major poets of the period *c.* 1373-1390, Chaucer, Gower or Langland, consult these formal studies of the function of mind or soul for the purpose of giving 'scientific' authority to their own poetic representations of psychological activity, or even for helping them in forming views on the activity of mind? Let us consider Gower first, for during the period when Langland was in the process of evolving the B-Text or had recently finished it, Gower as a London poet had been frightened out of his wits by the events of the summer of 1381, especially events which took place in his own parish. The result of his perturbation and moral indignation was a *visio* poem written in medieval Latin elegiac couplets. Many of the targets for Gower's didactic criticism (after the initial nightmare had passed) were those of Langland. But the artistic method in both framing the dream-activity and projecting the author's state of mind and mental process in personifications is quite distinct in the *Vox Clamantis* from Langland's usage in *Piers Plowman*. For one thing, Gower chooses to frame his dream-vision within the explicitly trance state of the Revelations of St John the Divine (*Vox Clamantis*, Prologue 56-59). Though the heart of the poet is disturbed with terror, Gower deliberately uses the scriptural 'revelation' as a controlling muse, stressing the biblical, hence 'true' and 'rational', nature of the poetic discourse. He goes out of his way to suppress the subjective and personal aspect of his dream appearance and experience. The Prologue to Book II, however much a modesty *topos*, still calls attention to the rational activity of the poet: his conscious selection and appropriation of images and words 'not his own'. He functions like the Lucretian bee, buzzing from poet to poet, passage to passage, lifting and taking away the flowery essence of others. This account is fairly close to the truth. The poem provides good evidence for Gower's direct and detailed reading of passages in Ovid which lie mainly outside the compass of the *Metamorphoses* (a poem widely drawn on in the *Confessio Amantis*). Gower in only one or two places in Book I comments on his state of mind. For example, in I. i. 146 ff. he says:

Prima quies aberat, ne adhuc mea lumina mulcet
Sompnus, quem timide mentis origo fugat.
En coma sponte riget, tremit et caro, cordis et antrum
Soluitur, *et sensus fertur ad instar aque.*
Sic magis assidua iactatus mente revolui,
Quid michi tam subiti causa timoris erat:
Sic lecto vigilans meditabar plura, *que mentem*
Effudi, variis corde vagante modis.

The expression in this passage is wholly controlled by well-tested
clarity of literary vocabulary and imagery. The italicized details ('my
senses were stirred to flowing much like water'; 'my mind wandered
abroad by diverse ways') are precise but hardly vivid. The image of
mental disturbance being compared to agitated water reminds one of
biblical similitude: Gower is recalling Psalm (Vulgate) 21.15: 'Sicut
aqua effusus sum', just as the *Gawain*-poet had in *Pearl* 365: 'As
wallande water got3 out of welle'. Similarly, the wandering of the
mind in various directions may distantly recall Lamentations 3.9.
Gower gives us another image of mental disturbance in chapter 16.
1427-8:

Sic mea sompniferis liquefiunt pectora curis,
Ignibus appositis vt nova cera solet:

The notion that his 'heart melted like fresh wax in approaching
flames' again shows the influence of Psalm 21.15: 'Factum est cor
meum sicut caera liquescens ...', but the phrase 'vt nova cera solet'
shows that the Psalmic memory has been blended with Ovid, and
where Ovid emerges as the dominant allusion. Compare *Epistulae Ex
Ponto* I. 2. 55-56:

Sic mea perpetuis liquefiunt pectora curis
    Ignibus admotis ut nova cera solet.
My heart melts from unending sorrows as fresh wax
is wont to do when fire is brought near.

In trying to appropriate the whole couplet unit from Ovid, Gower has
merely substituted *somniferis* for *perpetuis* and *appositis* for *admotis*. But
the isolated images are not particularly revealing of any psychological
or mental process. Throughout the poem the poet is the guardian of
conscience and the voice of reason (however distressfully crying out in
the wilderness), rather than the participant in the political and social

scenes of unrest and violence. The poet is often frightened, saddened and threatened but there is no real reflection of 'mentality' in the poem. In any case, only Book I is actually concerned with the proper material of a *visio*:

Vix ego quod potui cognoscere si fuit extra
Corpus quod vidi; seu quod ab intus erat.

(I. xx. 2055-6)

After this, the verses address themselves to social and moral criticism, and a didacticism of a particularly wearisome length and monotony of tone.

When we turn to the *Confessio Amantis* we are not on much more interesting ground for the study of literary representations of states of mind or processes of thought. Gower may call on 'Anglica Carmente metra iuuante loquar' and to a certain extent if we follow Servius (*ad Aeneid* VIII.336) she and Gower are concerned with the past and the future, especially the future state of England, and in the 'Richardian' version the future behaviour of the king. Even the mythological 'past' is deliberately historicized and euhemeristically treated. But Gower's penchant for the encyclopaedic mode is nearly all pervasive. The process of poetic recording becomes various aspects of exemplification: even the most personal feelings are transmuted into the exemplary: 'That every man ensample take/Of wisdom which him is betake ... and [I] therefore/Woll wryte and schewe al openly ...' (I.75 ff.). Whatever complexities of the psychological order are involved in the confessional exchanges and moral architectonics derived from that mixture of formality and intimacy which takes place or took place in the confessional—if we are all that persuaded by the obliquities and sleights-of-mind which Gower manipulates in repatterning the 'envelope' structure borrowed from Jean de Meun and his use of the consciousness (deserved or undeserved) of guilt in the original confessional situation. Jean de Meun seems much less taken in by the seriousness of the confessional than Gower who cannot quite abandon himself to literary irony or parody. Behind the encyclopaedic form[6] lies a further layer of instinctive reception of 'matere' itself derived from compendia, redactions and encyclopaedias.[7] The only literary area relatively free of his derivative working-habits is his first-hand appreciation of Ovid, especially the *Metamorphoses*.[8] But of the psychological side of Ovid's perception and art, The *Heroides* and *Amores,* there is little evidence of first-hand experience and deep appreciation. In the *Confessio* there is a dreary and thoroughly conventional account of the five senses (I. 300 ff.) where they are called 'gates to the heart'—a phrase which turns out to have homiletic origins (*Ayenbite of Inwit* 204/8). Book seven, testimony to the poet's wider interest in 'universal' learning, turns out to be a diluted and simplified version of a faintly 'Aristotelian-organized' compilation based partly on Bruno Latini's *Trésor* and other accounts. His conventional summary accounts of the four complexions, the heart as the seat of reason (VII. 484 ff.) and the place and function of the soul (Augustinian in drift rather than Aristotelian) do not rise above the most commonplace. Gower can hardly wait to arrive at *Philosophia Practica,* political science as he understood it, for it has a direct bearing on government and kingship. It is the heart of his mirror for princes. The author's deep and abiding philosophical interests lie here, in social and moral government and behaviour, based on the preceptual model of the conventional manuals of statecraft (VII. 1641 ff.). Occasionally, in this area, there is more departure from the *Trésor* and a genuine attempt to incorporate more heterogeneous material drawn from a wider selection of sources, some traceable to real historiography.[9] But in the main, Gower is an inveterate borrower from compilations. There is little evidence of settled reading or digested learning; there is abundant evidence of continuous recourse to digest and redactions.

Before one leaves Gower, something should be said about the *Mirroir de l'Omme.* Its schematic and encyclopaedic structure is based on religious models, *summae,* less encouraging for the representation of mentality or rational processes. I do not believe it will repay detailed analysis in the search for psychological vocabulary or images of the workings of mind. There is a passage (1609 ff.) which indicates that Gower is not overly fond of intellectual inquiry, or he at least misrepresents St Bernard so that a false antithesis is struck between the knowledge of 'self' and 'other things' ('l'autre vie'). In any case, Bernard's 'stude cognoscere te' or the old gnomic γνῶθι σεαυτόν means different things to different philosophical systems.[10] Like Langland, Gower indulges in detailed and realistic satiric descriptions of abuses ('triches') indulged in by all the 'estates', and the poet is most effective when dealing with drapers, goldsmiths, apothecaries, furriers, bakers, butchers, and vintners. There is even the occasional dramatic speech (25290 ff.). As a moral philosopher Gower is strong on 'mesure' (16536 ff.) and he has much to say on this virtue. But the interplay, no matter how complicated or how allegorized between vices and virtues cannot be adapted to psychological activity or internal deliberation. The summa-type personification of moral forces and immoral impulsions is unable to show the operations of individual minds or single processes. Its artistic programme begins from another direction and ends with a representation arrived at by conventions which estimate causes and effects in terms of already objectified and depersonalized forces. The mode of expression cannot be reconverted into the original thought of the writer. His concern for individuals and estates is 'reformation' and his own method (mental or psychological) of arriving at his moral purpose leaves no record of its participation in the act of rhetorical creation. Other 'minds' as well as his own process of thinking were never self-consciously involved in his mimetic inventions in the first place.

When we turn from Gower to his London-based contemporary, Chaucer, we are not in another city in another century, but certainly we are in a wholly different literary *quartier.* The reader's area of consciousness of the 'personality' and 'mentality' of the *auctor,* the self-conscious author, is not just much changed, but changed radically. In the three dream-poems, the *Book of the Duchess,* the *House of Fame,* and the *Parliament of Fowls,* the dimension of internal deliberation, emotional participation and mental process is openly exploited by the poet in a way which takes the reader of the poem into the authorial confidence. Chaucer never uses these displays of internality as 'ironical' play or masterly expositions of conscious attitudes for their own sakes. All his use of mental perspective is designed to give the whole poem a developing coherence and distribution of aesthetic emphasis in which proportion and *dispositio* and *ornatus* are achieved through a controlled and sustained invention of allusive elegance. Of course, in the development of his art and widening of his reading experience, the sources of the knowledge of mental processes and of the styles available to register them change and undergo enlargement and revision. But the fundamental quality of poetic intelligence and professional competence is not affected. In the early *Book of the Duchess* it is clear from the limitation in allusion, that the poet has not yet read and assimilated either of Alan of Lille's poetic works, the *De Planctu Naturæ* or the *Anticlaudianus,* yet the author shows an original and penetrating interest in the concepts of Nature and Moderation. The major field of concentration of these two concepts is mentality, psychological process which embraces the poles of reasoning and emotional distress.

The aesthetic problem of 'privateness' and 'generalness' of poetic or written expression, authorial reflection and dream experience, Chaucer has already solved by his understanding Macrobius's categories of dream analysis and types of literary invention as discussed in the *Commentum*. The 'solution' is put to artistic work by representing the internality of authorial deliberation and choice within the construction of the dream-poem. Inclusion ensures continuity and depth as well as relationship and perspective. Mimetic 'problems' are not concealed but are intimately related to processes of authorial deliberation and reflection, sometimes presented as comic, simplistic, or partially 'narrative'—as part of the ostensible plot. Although the reader knows that the poem is the result of periods of composition and revision, the dream-narrative is often 'misrepresented' as actual 'dream' not composition—most effectively at the end of the poem:

> Thoghte I, "This ys so queynt a sweven
> That I wol, be processe of tyme,
> Fonde to put this sweven in ryme
> As I kan best, and that anon."
> This was my sweven; now hit ys doon.

(1330-34)

Yet Chaucer occasionally steps outside his dream-experience (as at lines 95-100) to comment not only on the finished 'poem' but also to reflect on the emotional effect of the dream episode on the poet long after the waking period, long after, possibly, the period of composition:

> Such sorowe this lady to her tok
> That trewly I, which made this book,
> Had such pittee and such rowthe
> To rede hir sorwe, that, by my trowthe,
> I ferde the worse al the morowe
> Aftir, to thenken on hir sorwe.

The economy and conciseness of this observation does not in the least distract from the dominant experiental mood of narrative expression. At the same time, the author's observation on his own personal mood is not limited to himself, but is meant to be extended to the experience of the fictive 'John of Gaunt' as well, since that personage has already been defined as a projection of the author's consciousness and dream 'subconsciousness'; just as the insomnia and melancholia is shared both by creator and created character, one 'sorwe' in his 'imaginacioun', the other 'sorwe' in his 'herte'. This is not just a display of personal emotion but is more a general reflection on the limitations of reconcilement to grief and to the final value of resignation—although desirable and beneficial as 'philosophy' or mental health, but ineffective as an immediate cure to the depth and intensity of our natural feelings. Even the fictive time, 'al the morowe Aftir' is a figurative statement and is hardly meant to be taken literally. Loss of morbidity of mood and mind in poet and 'knight' emerges from the process of the act of dreaming and the identical act of composition. All the stages of this process are shared with the reader through various manipulations of mimetic techniques. The rhetorical *inventio* is subtle and substantial. Although the total design, the *archetypus,* of the *Book of the Duchess* is profoundly original, none of the poet's stratagems would have appeared mysterious or obscure to his classical authors (mainly Ovid) or to his friend Froissart, or to the poet of an older generation, Machaut.

After the sustained and psychologically elaborate use of the 'bedtime reading' *topos* in the *Book of the Duchess,* the *Parliament of Fowls* shows a more concise and philosophically directed use of the pre-sleep presentation of the conflict between the authority of literary text and the unsatisfied experience of the author-figure. Psychological process in this poem is curtailed, for the Chaucerian internal deliberation centres almost wholly within the circuit of problems initiated in the *Somnium Scipionis:* the relationship of *eros* and *agape* and the negativism of the Ciceronian adaptation of neo-Platonism with its denial of any positive value in natural human affection between man and woman. 'Almost', for the dreaming Chaucer's hesitation before the entrance to Venus's Temple, Scipio Africanus's rebuke and the shoving in of the reluctant poet (recalling Dante and his source, Virgil's *Æneid* VI) suggests, if obliquely, that the application has some grounding in authorial personal experience. It is not just an intellectual misunderstanding. Nevertheless, the dream substantially embodies and unfolds Chaucer's mental conflict and deliberation at the level of philosophical involvement. There is no need for the exemplary and transitional use of an intercalated *narratio* such as the Ceyx and Alcyone episode. The plot-structure of the *Parliament,* more closely modelled on Boccaccio's *archetypus* abstracted from the *Amorosa Visione,* achieves a perfect mimetic unfolding of the Chaucerian mental experience of a central ethical dilemma. This is why Chaucer is so anxious at the end of the poem-dream publically to appear to 'disown' his artistic success—to suggest that the topic will require further study and reflection and supplementary reading. A penchant for suspensive endings only partially explains Chaucer's concluding device; modesty also plays a part.

In the intermediate dream-poem, the *House of Fame*, the mentality of the poet-figure occupies an intermediate position. Chaucer is less an observer of dream-experience (as in the *Parliament*), moving more into the role of participant (as in the *Book of the Duchess*). The structure of the *House of Fame* shows a startlingly original use of the 'journey beyond' *topos* and a penetrating appreciation of Dantean architectonics of a kind which eludes Boccaccio's encyclopedic use of exemplary descriptive material reflecting Dantean style in the *Amorosa Visione*. Boccaccio captures the surface texture of Dante without in the least understanding his formal inventiveness. Chaucer's radical revamping of the pre-sleep experience in the *House of Fame* alerts the reader to the self-conscious nature of the dream-experience to come: the author's constant preoccupation with the poet's craft—not only thematic possibilities but the more important question of artistic motivation itself.

The inquisitive dream-investigator of the Venus Temple in book I undergoes a sudden change in status at the end of the Virgilian based tableaux with their disturbing emphasis on *Æneid* IV, the epyllion of Dido. The universal and unrelieved sterility of the *Deserta Libyæ* turns Chaucer into a full participant in the dream landscape, a part of its sinister solitude, its nothingness. His mental state is one of terror and anxiety, and we realize without benefit of commentary that all the dimensions and details of the dream are extensions of the poet's mental experience, past and present. They are the unexamined and unresolved problems and mental preoccupations of the pre-sleep, waking Chaucer, the poet Chaucer. The poet's fearfulness is fully appreciated by Gavin Douglas in book I of his *Palice of Honoure* and adapted there to the young writer's need.[11] As the *House of Fame* develops thereafter, the poet-dreamer's mental process is rendered in terms of conversational exchange and a renewed and enlarged form of a guided tour of nature. Wonder and creative perplexity succeed fear and anxiety. A wealth of unexpected 'realism' and variety of natural and imaginative experience replaces the emptiness of the Courts of Love. Though our manuscript tradition leaves us with a 'defective ending' to the poem,[12] yet we need no *conclusio* to explain to us how Chaucer's reworking of *Purgatorio* IX has rescued the creative mind from the 'fantom and illusioun' of a certain aspect and kind of poetry and the pride and ambition of others. We also know that he is safe from the unhealthy blandishments of the goddess Fama. The poem is the record of an internal aesthetic struggle, as intense in its own way as the long psychological struggle registered in the *Pearl*.

We do not need, I think, to prolong this survey into the already well analyzed dramatic and tragic creation of states of mind in the *Book of Troilus* or the complex and ironical use of psychological 'realism' in the *Canterbury Tales* to prove Chaucer's professional interest in the literary representation of 'mentality'. It seems to me that Chaucer's knowledge of mental processes and states of emotion is not derived chiefly from scientific and technical discussions (whether Aristotelian or Augustinian) or primarily from compilations and *compendia* (as in the case of Gower). His poet's understanding derives directly from observed experience and his accurate and searching reading of literature, whether mental states be represented by Virgil or Ovid, Dante or Boccaccio, or Froissart, Machault or Deschamps. His more philosophical and speculative interests are, of course, partially represented by Alan of Lille and Boethius. With Chaucer we finally arrive in another literary world, an ambiance full of perspective, a richness and variety of opinions and impressions arrived at through an understanding of subjective assessment and the necessity to record that subjectivity. We can regard this authorial commitment as 'unmedieval' or 'unrepresentative' of fourteenth-century English poets, but his success in mastering the techniques and understanding the points of view of the 'olde poetrie' is representative of the continuous efforts made by medieval writers from the Carolingian period onwards to 'humanize' themselves, to achieve (however circumscribed) some form of literary *renascentia*. John of Salisbury's *Metalogicon* describes the educative programme which made possible this liberating, humanistic process in moving detail.

The literary quarter of Langland's London (however distortedly it reflects the mixed commercial, criminal and ecclesiastical milieu of the Cornhill ward) presents the medieval reader with a very different view of mental states and processes. For one thing, Langland is not in the least heir of a literary education. What his family guardians provided was more practical as well as basic. Beyond a small collection of Old French and Anglo-Norman authors and the basic curriculum text the *Dicticha Catonis* we have little impression of literary reading. His own familiar companions (besides the texts of his trade which he lists in Passus VI (C) 45-47) are more 'useful', the Vulgate, the liturgy, some patristic commentaries and homiletic writings. So, unlike Chaucer, Langland's experience of 'mentality' cannot *ab initio* derive from literature. Unlike Gower, Langland gives little sustained evidence of having been an assiduous consulter of *compendia*. But in the poet's interview with Anima in Passus XV we have incontrovertible evidence in ME and Latin that Langland had recourse to Isidore's encyclopaedia, the *Etymologiæ*, for Anima's direct account of itself. Langland's mention of both Augustine and Isidore shows he was aware of Isidore's source in the *De Spiritu et Anima* I. 34. Thus, there is a strong Augustinian colouring to Langland's theoretical knowledge of the Isidorian paradigm of the concept of Anima. But whether this proves ultimately of pronounced significance in a full account of Langland's appreciation of 'mind' is another matter. The peculiar arrangement of the series of interviews in the poem with the essentially disconnected functions or 'faculties' of the author's own mind from Passus VIII onwards makes it almost impossible for the reader to experience these internal powers or mental functions in a pattern which might suggest a coherent integration of 'personality' or character. Even when extracted from the digressive movements and thematic ruminations of the questioning *narratio*, the various *vis* often repeat functions and nearly always show a tendency in dramatic personification to become aspects of the poet's conscious attitudes or obsessions. In other words, it is not a systematic presentation of a dreaming or fictive mentality, although the self-definition by Anima makes a token gesture in the direction of systematization. One could more readily understand the poetic sacrifice of system if the scientific disorganization were then used to sustain the poetic coherence of the *narratio*, especially to point the direction of the psychological quest for self-education. But the narrative is less sustained than it had been earlier in the unit Prologue, Passus I-VII. We do not see the *vis* or *potentia animae* in any connecting *enfilade*. The poetic 'self' meets with a series of aspects of his mental 'self' which reflects equal or a greater state of incomplete understanding, or at times of being confused. The poetic self looks for guidance and instruction and usually finds greater wisdom or understanding in personages who are not demonstrably part of his mental selfhood—though it could be argued that these figures of educative authority (such as Trajan) must have passed through the poet's 'mental' apprehension and been stored in his *memoria* or otherwise they could not have entered his dream-world in the first place. But this is a circular form of proof and does not shed any real light on the poetic or scientific patterning of the poem or on the poetic intelligence responsible for the artefact in the relation of parts to whole.

Whatever the strength of cases for or against the separation of the poem into *visio* (Prologue, Passus I-VII) and *vita* (Passus VIII-XX), there is a distinct difference in the presentation of authorial mentality between the *visio* and the *vita*. The inwardness of the *vita* contrasts strongly with the externality of the *visio*, especially as regards the rendering of the authorial process of mind. In the *visio* unit the state of mind of the creator of the poem is not substantially or systematically presented: in general the relation of the dreamer-poet to his own mental process or reflective experience has neither inwardness nor deliberativeness. The significance of events in the dream-world or why they should occur in any particular sequence does not deeply disturb or otherwise engage the dreamer's sustained curiosity. From time to time he may require instruction or seek advisement. This usually takes the shape of a formal exchange, hermeneutic in tone and neutral in emotional content. Contradictions, disagreements, and dilemmas usually take place either between representative personages or personfications, or as the argumentative monologue of such figures, only occasionally traceable to human process of mind, e.g., Conscience, Reason etc., and these figures are more usually not emphatically linked to the authorial mind. The enactment of contradictions and solutions of problems are all part of the externalized, representative social drama. The authorial psychological vocabulary is, on the whole, simple, direct and uncomplicated. In the Prologue the following selection is typical: 'I behelde' (13), 'I seigh' (14), 'fonde I' (17), 'I seigh' (50), 'I fond' (58), 'I perceyved' (100), 'I seiȝ' (217), 'seiȝ I' (230). Perhaps only the verb 'perceyven' (which may include the process of realization) introducing us to the notion of the Cardinal Virtues and their relation to 'love' and 'scholarship', is intended especially to call the reader's attention to an area of special concern to Langland the poet.

With Passus I the poet becomes less an observer and more of a participant, or at least partner in a dialogue. Since we are alerted to 'meaning' (lines 1-2) we should expect to find definite signs of interpretative activity. The iteration of the adjective 'faire' (2, 4) which links Langland's intention and Holy Church's manner of address indicates the poet's concern for clarity and economy of poetic discourse, e.g., by transferring the adjective to adverbial function:

Þe felde ful of folke, I shal ʒow faire schewe.

The request for 'explantion' (11) is met by prescriptive exhortation with the emphasis on 'mesurable manere' (19). The mental activities required of the dreamer are simple: '*rekne* hem bi resoun' (22), and '*reherse* þow hem after'. Enumeration and repetition implies the process of memorization which creates a state of awareness ('þow sholdest ben ywar', (42). The process of memorization leads to an essentially defensive, cautious state of mind; the learning process reinforces preceptual, authoritative values. The poet-figure behaves as if he were perfectly satisfied. There are no overt signs of reluctance or discontent. The imagery which follows (lines 54 ff.), the rule of reason, the natural intelligence as 'guardian'—the figurative sense is borrowed from a social institution—implies that the dreamer is under obligation to show obedience, as if he were not yet qualified for full responsibility. Similarly, in the phrase 'tutour of ʒoure tresore', an educational sense may also be included in the application of the noun *tutour*. Subsequent usages of Holy Church reflect the instructional, educative and institutionalized application of the mind to the problem of moral awareness, e.g., 'vnderfonge' and 'tauʒte feyth'. In line 77, the phrase, 'broughtest me borowes' (the promises of the sponsor on behalf of the newly baptized) also implies dependence as well as incapability. Instructional references and institutional practices reinforce the simplicity, the directness of moral reflection (line 92: 'knoweþ/kenne it aboute'). The activity of knights ends with arrests and a legal metaphor with 'Trewthe' as a judge 'ytermed [their] trepas' (97). The accumulation of institutional images after line 105 culminates in another educative verb (109): 'Tauʒte hem bi þe trinitee treuthe to knowe'. The educative emphasis is unmistakable: 'lerned' (111), 'bi siʒte of þise texts' (132), 'lereth' (134), 'kenne' (136), 139 ff., 'teche' (143), 'lere' (144), 'lered' (149) etc. Needless to say, the dramatic nature of the relationship of the dreamer to Holy Church accounts for much of the instructional nature of the imagery. But one suspects that the proclivity for the educative verbs and images goes deeper than dramatic personification: it is part of the fundamental experience of the creative mind, and the natural expression of its activity in any process of cognition.

The evidence of the next Passus supports the consistent use of educative in verbs relation to cognition, or the apprehension of external experience: 'Kenne me to knowe' (II.7), 'construeth' (36), 'wit' (44), 'This text telleth þe' (121); 'Crist knoweþ þi conscience' (III. 67), 'I lere yow' (III. 69). In Passus IV the legal nature of the narrative action determines much of the range of the verbal activity but there is no radical shift in emphasis: 'rede' (of Resoun) (IV. 5, 9), 'lernest þe people' (of Conscience) (IV. 11), 'knewe' (of Conscience) (31, 41), 'knewe' (of the king) (61). These verbs of knowing represent simple acts of 'recognition' of the truth of something, of the nature of someone, or of being acquainted with someone socially (fig.), so of Pees (IV. 80) 'þe comune knowen þe sothe'; 'yseiȝen' (of the author's experience of his last dream) (V. 4), 'saw I' (of the author's present dream) (V. 9), 'I shall seye as I saw' (of the author's truth of experience) (V. 22) etc. In Passus VII a certain variation occurs in connection with mental activity mainly in the 'epilogue' (lines 142 ff.): 'to study of þat I seigh slepyng' (142), 'ful pensyf in herte' (145),—this is syntactically ambiguous, it might refer to either Piers or to the author, 'sauoure in songwarie' (148), 'makeþ me ... to thynke' (167). None of these uses of verbs and associated phraseology is particularly striking or very revealing of introspection. Langland's poetic method (accumulative, satiric, personificative, condensed, instructional, heavily dependent on institutional analogies and textual authority) tells us little about individual mental processes or about any special theory of mental activity. Recognition ('to know') is the most frequent formulation and very much in tune with the patristic, Augustinian and Cassiodorian theory in the independent preexistence of abstract Ideas (originating in the Mind of God) which we in turn experience by recognition and so automatically assent to. Elaborate processes of reasoning or the exercise of logic are not particularly necessary to the reformation of one's attitudes or to the changing of one's opinions.

The reader should be alerted early in Passus VIII that a change will occur in the presentation of authorial mentality. Lines 20-56 contain a quasi-satiric version of a dispute between the author-figure (awake) and a friar, conducted on the one side (the poet's) by a set-piece of chop-logic in which the necessary truth of the major premise is denied in all cases and therefore need not be true in any particular case. It is answered by an *argumentum ab similitudine* (Augustinian in origin) of elaborate silliness by the friar. Nothing whatever comes of this exchange and the 'disputants' take their leave with exaggerated civility. However 'formal' and satiric it does signal a change in emphasis—a movement towards an interest in reasoning. On falling asleep, the first figure the poet meets is not a personification of the kind with which he had met in the first section of the poem. He meets a figure who not only knows him personally (calls him by name) and is eager to engage him in conversation, but who is his own 'thought', part of his mentality. This figure has nothing whatever to do with memory and critical attempts to precisely define the mental function of this 'thought' are bound to prove unsatisfactory. Langland's tendency in the case of his presentation of each 'faculty' is to use the *vis animae* as a 'beginning-motif', as a method of introducing material for further discussion and enlargement. In this case, the introducing mental power is in its poetic infancy. When we are introduced to 'Wit' after line 113, it would seem that, although Thought and Wit are to be distinguished as functions (comparing their physical characteristics) yet they are not distinguished as personifications in terms of their speech or the content of their thought, only in degree of knowing. Wit knows the location of Dowel, Thought does not. Thought is a 'moche man' and 'lyke to myselve', which is hardly surprising. The exchange serves to introduce the grammatical metaphor of Dowel, Dobet, Dobest in a hierarchical arrangement characterised by institutional associations. But these expositions of the three figures are basically associational, although the poet and his Thought spend three days disputing about Dowel. One supposes that the emphasis on Dowel signifies that Thought knows best about the most straightforward of the trio. The conversation (or as much as we are allowed to be privy to) is characterised by didactic or educative vocabulary: *wisse, knowe, tauȝte, lerne*—a tendency carried over from the first section of the poem, from the *visio*. No new technique has been devised. The associative functions and personified activities assigned to Dowel, Dobet, Dobest are difficult to assess as definable forms of 'knowing about' entities. Definition in Langland proceeds nearly always by accumulation, a process of gradual figural accretion, repetition and augmentation. Some of these accretic details are not always easy to translate into the cold prose of rational statement—often when so translated or paraphrased the statement is about as interesting as the highway code. Having embarked upon a political and monarchial metaphor (lines 98 ff.), Langland makes very heavy weather of the absolutism of Dobest by introducing the possibility of Dowel and Dobet acting against Dobest in some unspecified way:

Þanne shal þe kynge come and casten hem in yrens,
And but if Dobest bede for hem, þei to be þere for euere.

But this is not only confusing but illogical in view of the grammatical foundation of the trio metaphor and ethical implications of the metaphoric terminology. In any case, who exactly is the 'kynge'? Is this a secular analogy and if so, what is the analogous referent? One notices that Langland's editors fall silent on this passage. In the C-Text this troublesome piece of bad thinking has been removed, though the revamped poetic expression is flat and without energy. We cannot place all the blame on the dreaming poet-figure's Thought. The short and relatively uncomplicated Passus VIII gives way to a more elaborate and expansive Passus IX largely narrated by the second of Langland's mental powers, Wit.

Wit would appear to be some more active process of 'understanding', though it cannot be identified with the result of thinking, 'knowledge' or 'understanding', in the sense of something arrived at, 'knowledge'.[13] Langland's Wit is an active personage who appears suddenly out of the blue (114). He too resembles the poet, long and lean, a complete 'individual' (if that is what 'liche to none othere' means). His appearance and activity is initially that of a 'moderator'. In other words, he has an ethical bias, a moral nature. Cassiodorus divided the soul's powers into moral and natural. The soul's moral power is exerted through the Four Cardinal Virtues. Langland may have borrowed this moral aspect from Cassiodorus. As we have not been told the substance of Langland's argument about the nature of Dowel with Thought it is impossible to judge what exactly Wit is going to be the 'mene bitwene' (if that is what the grammar means here). Langland ends by asking quite another question, namely, the distinction between the Dowel, Dobet, Dobest trio. Thought turns the responsibility of answering this poser over to Wit.

Building on the personification-metaphor of thought (VIII. 123 ff.), Wit engages on a long, schematic similitude or allegory of the 'domus' or residence type, very familiar to the medieval reader (the parallel drawn with a passage in the *Ancrene Wisse* is but one amongst many). Wit is not very accurate about the composition of the body out of the four elements, getting one element wrong ('fire' has been omitted). I do not think that by 'eyre' Langland can have meant the *aether* since 'pure' or 'bright', it cannot be equated with the ele-

ment of 'fire'. I do not see why Langland could not have been influenced by an intrusive memory of Genesis 2.7, however he chose to
translate *spiraculum* elsewhere in the poem.[14] The Castle of 'Mankind'
(Langland does not name it) evokes a household similitude in which
Anima is the Lady, Kynde (creating Nature, soon to merge into God
at line 26 ff.) is the Lover, Sir Dowel, lord of the manor and protector
of Anima, Dobet is Anima's Lady Companion and daughter to
Dowel, Dobest is some churchman who ranks with a bishop and who
is spiritual advisor to Anima. Strangely, he also seems to have power
over the manorial lord in the district who, presumably, only leases the
castle. The castle has a constable or governor responsible for security
who is called Inwit. This must be taken in the sense 'mind'—all the
mental powers (cf. *MED minde*, n.) (17) for by his first wife he has
begot the five senses. Langland is not accurate about these either.
Sight, speech and hearing are secure but 'Worche-wel-wyth-thine-
hande', is doubtfully touch, and the fifth sense, 'Sire Godfrey Gowel'
indicates that perhaps Langland has confused two categories
originating in Cassiodorus's *De Anima*. In this account the natural
powers of the soul are five in number. The first power is 'sensible'
(the five senses), the second power is 'imperative' and governs cor-
poral motion.[15] This might explain 'Gowel'. The expression 'first
wife' suggests that by a second marriage Inwit has had the five inward
wits (commonsense, imagination, fancy, estimation and memory).
Langland's learning is not exact or systematically sound. He
sometimes appears more learned than he actually is. The main emphasis in the domus similitude remains upon education ('Anima that
lady is ladde by his *lerning*'). The network of relationships is both
familiar and feudal. There is created an interesting sense of qualifica-
tion and interdependence, though the household imagery remains
static and finds no extensive application beyond its own iconography.
It is probably the social aspect of these images which interested the
poet most, and marriage and work are the clearest images to emerge
of Dowel. The ethical concern of Wit is most pronounced in his em-
phasizing of the protective, proscriptive aspects of moral and physical
obedience. The moral code (line 199-206) reinforced the earlier
similitudes but also encloses a considerable amount of satiric and
critical observations on the relations of men and women. This is not
especially well-written and perhaps signals that the poet's imagination
is already moving into a satiric weather-system which will produce the
extended squalls of the next Passus. The problem for the literary critic

is not one of understanding the message but of estimating how successful Langland has been in hybridizing the imaginative inventions, the similitudes, with the 'philosophical' schemes (such as they are). It can hardly be said that the emergent ethical study is very interesting or original, and the poetic rendering of Wit and Wit's reasoning also lacks memorableness. As Dr Johnson once remarked in another context: 'one would rather praise it than read it.' The poetry of Passus IX seems to rise between two stools. An initial interest in mentality soon yields to ethical definition and social criticism. We are all the time slipping back into the mode of the first section of the poem without the formal clarity and emphatic rhythm of the *visio*.

The beginning satiric energy of Passus X cannot be ignored. Wit's sober definition of the form and purpose of Christian marriage and his angry strictures on those who show little heed of the proper end of matrimony are brilliantly and bitterly answered by the appearance of Wit's own wife, Dame Study. She is a memorable creation, worthy of employ at any Dotheboy's Hall in Yorkshire, a vivid refutation in the flesh of the careful questioning, moral rectitude and earnest concern of authorial mentality displayed in the last two Passus. With the invention of Wit's wife, the poet escapes for a time from his own plan of successive meetings with his own mental powers, of a manifestly orderly progression of self-educative quest. The outburst of stored-up, vitriolic force creates a memorable diatribe and portrait, but it does little to help the coherence of the *narratio*. Coherence is not aided either by Langland's habitual recourse to a single type of sequential pattern: the serial introducing of interviews between the dreamer-author and a personification. The same fault may be traced back to Jean de Meun's continuation of the *Roman*. Dame Study would appear to be an original creation of Langland's. I cannot remember a similar invention elsewhere in ME, OF or medieval Latin. Alan of Lille briefly personified *Studium* (= 'thought directed to the accomplishment of a purpose', 'zealousness') in Book IX. 305 of the *Anticlaudianus* ('Studium fugat Occia') where the emphasis is favourable. Langland's figure presumably is a personification of 'the application of the mind to the activity of leaning'. Her hollowness of face, leanness of body, fierce, unbending stare are but a prelude to her withering dismissal of her husband—mocking, taunting, mixing Latin tag (*noli mittere*), the proverbial ('margerye-perlis Amanges hogges'), cutting verbs ('dryuele') and a forceful impetus of syntax and rhythm which fairly take the breath away. Ignoring the poet, save to insinuate that he may be one of the 'fools' or 'sottes', she moves on to launch a blistering attack on the state of contemporary theological learning and dispute. Her depth of analysis of intellectual corruption is not as important as the compelling force and reforming intensity of this coruscating exposé. Her words are a continuous flow of intemperance of expression (down to line 132) which reduces poor old Wit to state of confused silence, physical shrinking ('drowe him arere') and simulated laughing obedience. It is as if lawyer Jaggers were suddenly turned into the aged P. By obsequious gestures Wit persuades the poet to address Dame Study, and after an equally obsequious promise of obedience and intellectual servitude from the poet (only toadies need apply), Dame Study with sublime inconsistency becomes obligingly helpful and promises to hand the poet on to her cousin 'Clergie'. Earlier in the poem (Prologue 116, Passus III.15) we had briefly come across this noun. In the Prologue the meaning should perhaps be the educated high ecclesiastics who sat with the lords temporal in parliament; the same force probably applies to the passage in Passus III, for we are still in the ambiance of Westminster, though it is not clear that the noun in III.15 should be regarded as a personification. Here, in the description of 'Clergie' which follows, we should extend the sense to include the schools and universities—and so the figure which Langland will meet next is 'Learning'. Again, it must be observed we are moving away from 'mentality' and introspection into the didactic and satiric methods habitually employed by Langland. 'Ymaginatyf' and 'Anima' are a long way off.

Educative verbs and nouns continue to be used and the old familiar imagery continues to connect 'Learning' to 'Study' and 'Scripture' as wife to Clergie and 'sybbe to þe seuene artȝ'. But one wonders, how is this relationship to be imagined? Why are Clergie and Scripture but recently married (six months in A and B; edited away in C). Perhaps, this signifies that the union has not yet had time to bear fruit or perhaps they have not yet had time to fall out. Either way, Langland cannot be wrong. The enumeration of various bits of the *Artes* (171-9) is perfunctory and mixed with practical skills which have no place in the scheme of the Seven Liberal Arts. Basically, Langland's Study is anti-intellectual, and morally reductive or simplifying (line 208: 'loue' as a 'science'). In her account of the quadrivium, sciences, pseudo-sciences and magic are all related and ultimately rejected. The same tendency may be glimpsed in the poet's imagining of

Clergie. The use of Augustine's *De Trinitate* after line 241 and the quotation in line 248 of St Gregory separates faith from reason and elevates faith at the expense of reason. The total effect of Clergie's instruction is prescriptive, fundamentalist and unexperimental. Clergie's and Study's attacks on 'scholarship' are plainly digressive and aimed at wide targets. I do not think we are entitled to see Langland alluding to various individual contemporary figures such as Robert Holcot, Thomas Buckingham, and Adam Woodham, however tempting it may be to do so.[16] Langland's personifications seem to object to, and criticize moral attitudes and ethical conduct rather than ideas and doctrines. He is closer to the old *Satura Communis* and its origins in Juvenal, than he is to the concerns of modern scholarship.

The overal effect of Passus X is accumulatingly depressing. It loses a programmatic direction towards self-education in gaining the brilliant but divertingly satiric and critical set-pieces and the portrait of Dame Study. Aside from Study's arresting opening metaphor of perverted instruction as a fuller's form teasing up the poor cloth into a semblance of pile and thick fibres, there is little vivid imagery or symbolism borrowed from institutions or different levels or programmes of learning. There is no detailed evidence of an informed criticism of ecclesiastical schools or the universities. Mentally we are never far from the resources of a mind with the experience of only a basic education. There is a passing and disapproving reference to the Abbot of Abingdon but no explicit reference to Oxford (not far distant) or to Cambridge. The confounding of Wit by Dame Study and the poet's being handed on to Clergie and Scripture only confuses and demoralises the poet-figure (cf. line 372). It drives the figure of Will further from the methods, sources and authorities of fourteenth-century learning, however the critics seek to explain this away.

Dejection and despair sit heavily upon the poet (Passus XI) as he is abused by Scripture and disparaged by the quotation of pseudo-Bernard: 'multi multa sciunt, et seipsos nesciunt'. It seems a little hard that the poet should be accused of want of self-knowledge for he has become the passive auditor-victim of a series of active, vocal forces who long ago silenced his Wit and have treated him to a confused medley of complaint, satire and exposition. But as these personifications belong properly to his own self and are the product of his own education, then, one can only suppose, he gets what he deserves. The subjective or objective status of Langland's personifications is invariably confused and both author and reader are hardly ever allowed to share an experience of dominant artistic perspective. The dream-within-a-dream must be the result of sorrow and anger and transports the poet (thanks to Dame Fortune) into a partially introspective and retrospective struggle of forty-five years of worldly temptation. Perhaps for the first time the author allows the reader to see a representation of his own sense of specific failure. In the Mirror of Middle Earth we expect to experience Langland's *crise de conscience* directly and visually. Alas, this does not happen. Instead, the dreamer divides himself up into another set of personifications, experiencing another set of interviews and dialogues. The poet appears to have had little trouble with *Concupiscentia-carnis* (this sorts well with his earlier perfunctory account of *Luxuria* in Passus V), but the younger sister of Fortuna, *Coueytise-of-eyes,* seems to have proved more than a handfull for all of the forty-five years (XI. 44-50). This is *concupiscentia oculorum* of I John 2.16 and she plainly identifies herself as the desire for worldly possessions (lands, manor houses, etc.). It would appear that as soon as the poet 'hastens towards old age' (59 ff.), all previous warnings come true—he experiences adversity, Mala Fortuna, and becomes poor. On reflection, it seems strange that this should convince us that we are reading anything other than a wholly fictive biography. Nothing that we know of the poet heretofore would suggest this pattern of experience, especially in view of the material contained in the C-Text, Passus VI, unless the C-Text material is entirely editorial. But whatever the degree of fictionalization,[17] here the poet suffers a series of spiritual crises which rapidly digresses into debates over baptism, salvation, the conflict of laws (ecclesiastical and natural) and the role of contrition. What appeared to be able to be made an interesting (if highly fictionalized 'autobiography') has been allowed to decline into the dull, digressive and diffuse. Whatever the reason for this inventive failure, the wayward movement of the narrative is halted by Trajan's indignant exclamation '3ee, baw for Bokes!' at line 135—and not about time, one feels.

Like Dante before him (cf. *Paradiso* XX. 43-5, 100 ff.), Langland seems to have had a special affection for the Emperor Trajan. Even the phrase: 'one was broken oute of helle' (135) seems to echo Dante's 'chè l'una dello inferno' (106) but we must not presume that Langland knew any of the *Commedia;* his knowledge would have originated in Jacobus ab Voragine's *Legenda Aurea* (cap. 46) in the life of St Gregory (acknowledged in lines 155 ff.). There are references in

Thomas Aquinas and elsewhere, but I do not think Langland was informed in any great detail about the specific arguments over 'heathen' salvation.[18] But the account in the *Legenda* is not 'larger than I ʒow telle' (155), whatever Trajan says. The real largeness of Langland's speech of Trajan lies in its magnificently clear exposition of 'loue and leute is a lele science'. The empty words of Dame Study are here given flesh and blood: the flesh and blood of Christ the *Redemptor*. Incarnation and Passion are related not only to 'law' and 'learning' but to Patience and Poverty—and, of course, to one of Langland's major preoccupations, activity: 'so bi his *workes* thei wisten that he was Iesus' (230). Of course, Trajan continues the anti-intellectual bias we have noted before but the Christocentric emphasis—its clear and uncomplicated anticipation of Passus XVIII and the last image of the poor, needy Christ in Passus XX, gives us a fuller understanding of the poet's possible answer to man's requirement of logic, 'reasoning', and disputation.

I would have wished for the sake of poetic emphasis and economy that the Passus had ended with Trajan's discourse and that some other transition to the next Passus had been invented. But Langland's dream is prolonged by a meeting with Kynde (Nature) who instructs him by visual examples and takes him on the traditional guided tour of terrestial creation. The wondrousness, plenitude and variety of Chaucer, Alan and Bernardus Sylvestris is unfortunately not represented by Langland's Nature or creation itself. In Langland Kynde is sexless and undescribed, and the wholesomeness of natural beauty is spoilt by a series of contrastive pairings (poverty/plenty, peace/war, bliss/bale, mede/mercy) introduced by 'Man and his make'. Langland, after a not unattractive tour of animal life, especially birds—though the poet does seem a little too preoccupied with reproductive functions—takes up the phrase 'Man and his make' again at line 362 and presumes to rebuke Reason for making only less 'man' unreasonable. Aristotelian biology seems to be unknown to Langland, who distributes rational souls or reasoning functions to animals in common with man so as to support the claim that man as a rational animal lacks the reasonableness of animals in sexual arrangements and domestic management (360-63). We have to wait for Lydgate for the first recorded English use of the noun 'instinct' in the biological context but historians of medieval Aristotelian thought assure us that Aristotelian distinctions about the distribution of rational souls were well-known in this and earlier periods and Vincent of Beauvais supplies ample supporting evidence. The poet imagines éducative programmes for all of natural creation: every creature knows by being taught ('Moche merueilled me what maister þei hadde/And who tauȝte hem...'). What is fictive in the *Parliament of Fowls* would be natural fact for Langland. The dreamer is rebuked by Reason, not for his animal biology, but for his neglect of Biblical argument supported by a quotation from 'Cato'. Covered with shame and blushing at Reason's rebuke, the poet wakes only to meet with the as yet unidentified Ymaginatyf who further lectures the poet on his philosophical presumption. He compares the poet's honest efforts at obtaining knowledge with the reason why Adam was expelled from Paradise (407-412). He will be accused in the same terms later by Anima.

With the beginning of Passus XII we have at long last returned to the main road of the poet's process of self-education. The meeting with, and questioning of, mental forces of his own being. The use of the adjectival form 'Ymaginatyf' in ME does not help to clarify the precise operation of this mental power in Langland. It is plain from the dictionary evidence that 'Imaginacioun', 'Imaginatif', and 'vertu imaginatif' share most, if not all definitions. I think Mr. Schmidt is right in rejecting the very narrow definition involving the purely mechanical transmission of images from the *sensus communis,* for Langland's 'faculty' plainly 'prompts' (XII.4) the poet to meditate on things past and things to come, possibilities (such as 'damnation') in the future. So we begin with the faculty as 'the ability to form images of past and future events'. The power is plainly not part of Anima's Augustinian definition of herself in Passus XV. Langland, though drawn to schemes and systems, remains ultimately unsystematic and perplexingly original.

We have commented earlier on the way in which the dramatic quality of Langland's personifying extends the poetic activity of Ymaginatyf beyond any simple technical definition. The activity ('I haue folwed þe in feith þis fyue and fourty wyntre') suggests the role of a family servant or steward, and perhaps may connect with Ymaginatyf's first quotation of Luke XII.38, where the cautionary words of Christ 'Si non in prima vigilia nec in secunda ...' end with the words 'blessed are those servants'. The 'hours' are imaginatively linked with the Three Ages of man mentioned in the lines before. The imaginative connection is long and well-known, beginning probably in Gregory the Great's *Homilies in the Evangelists* (Lib. I. Hom. 13) and spread via the *Glossa Ordinaria*.[19] The tone of Ymaginatyf's self-description as attendant and dutiful admonitor is gloomy, cheerless and denigratory of the art of poetry. This 'imaginative' power has nothing to do with the creative imagination of an artist. After the poet's lamentably weak attempt to defend the practice of poetry, Ymaginatyf takes up the poet's expressed wish to know about the nature of Dowel, Dobet, Dobest. From line 30 onwards a volley of sermonizing pours forth supported by a wealth of quotation and illustration. The style is that of a workman pounding nails in a packing-case. There is an interesting case made out for 'learning' by the Augustinian association of Christ's activity with 'writing' (79-84) which we have already commented on. Unfortunately, it is given a purely moral application (85-86) and left as a consolement for those who have repented. But Ymaginatyf persists and widens again the application of learning (lines 99 ff.), connecting 'inspiration' with the Holy Ghost, developing the 'coffre of Crystes tresore' backwards in time with the Old Testament and drawing a parallel with the *'Archa-dei* in þe Olde Lawe'. But the case is argued ever more remorselessly and the didactic tone wears out one's sympathy and interest. One's attention is aroused again when he arrives at nature and the question of animal 'knowledge'. He begins by putting the nature of animal behaviour beyond human learning or innate moral sense (224-6). Nature (who is masculine) alone 'knows', and then Ymaginatyf employs an arresting phrase:

He [Kynde] is þe pyes patroun and *putteth it in hire ere*
þat þere þe þorn is thikkest to buylden and brede.

> (227-8)
> [fol. 52a]

Does this approach near to some instinctual theory—a system of 'hints' or 'promptings', close to the function of *estimatio* in the human mind? The argument is immediately muddied by the use of the educative verb 'kenned' (applied both to peacocks and Adam). In line 235 he again seems to put even Adam's action in eating the apple beyond human reason: 'Kynde knoweth whi he ded so, ac no clerke elles'. But then the whole tenor of the argument shifts and we are off on a digression on the metaphorical or the emblematic use of animals (bestiary material basically). The reference to Aristotle in connection with the lark and moral similitude is, alas, mistaken. One feels there is almost an interesting and original theory hovering at the edges of the sermonizing, but that somehow Will's 'imaginative' power has missed the opportunity, or failed to see the implications. As in the case of Wit and Thought, the confrontation of the poet with some aspect of his mentality turns into an introductory motif—the poetry turns away from any process of internal realization to long sermonizing exhortations.

It is, of course, disquieting to find that having once again seemed to be embarked on a journey of self-discovery or attempted self-examination, one finds the itinerary halts only a few yards up the road. The accumulation of evidence as to nature of Dowel, Dobet, Dobest does not compensate for the evaporation of internal, psychological dimension. What is it that the dreamer is searching for? Does he know? The absence of any prominent passages in which the reader is taken into the authorical confidence during all this self-educative twisting and turning undermines the reader's confidence in the poet's ultimate, complete understanding of the *archetypus* and *dispositio* of the poem. It comes as somewhat of a shock to find that Passus XIII begins with the admission that there has been a long break in time ('many a ȝere after'), that the duration of the dreamer's experience or awareness of connected experience has been broken by a long period of living the life of a mendicant—during which time the poet has pondered much on the experiences of Passus XII. There follows a summary (not especially revealing) and memorable lines about the damaging power of uneducated parish priests:

> And how þat lewed men ben ladde (but owre lorde hem helpe)
> þorugh vnknonnyng curatoures to incurable peynes.

>   (12-15).
>   [fol. 53a]

The balancing of the negative adjectives, the *traductio* between 'curatours' and 'incurable', the continuous movement of the syntax leading to the *gradio* in the final noun 'peynes', demonstrates the poet's ability to create vivid satiric phraseology. But the temporal disconnection between Passus XII and Passus XIII seems somehow oddly symptomatic of the intermittent authorial control over the larger architectonics of the poem. Why should this 'fictional' break occur here? After the poet falls asleep again, it becomes apparent that the disconnection may have something to do with the fact that we have not returned to a process of self-discovery at all; and certainly, for the immediate future, 'cognition', 'mentality', 'inner process', confrontation of the authorial figure with aspects of self—none of this will come about. Instead, we are whisked away to a dinner party chez Conscience and treated to another long satiric extravaganza of the order of the earlier Dame Study digression. Some of the earlier characters (Clergie and Scripture) are invited too. The detailed account of the evening's entertainment (the food, the seating arrangements, the conversations, the ensuing arguments, the whispered asides and comments) is immensely amusing and yields an impressive portrait of the condescending, gluttonous, complacent, hypocritical 'Doctor' (presumably an Oxford- or Cambridge-trained scholar who holds high office in Church, Government or University). He is one of the few personages of the poem who invokes the author's active angry participation.

The dinner party breaks up but the satiric impulse which invented it persists for an extraordinary length of time. On the way home, Conscience, Patience and the poet meet by pure chance 'Activa-Vita' or Haukin, a minstrel and wafer-maker (amongst other things). Perhaps his name, a diminutive of Hal, suggests that we are entitled to see a punning reference both to peddling and the sport of hawking. Although not so initially amusing as the portrait of the gluttonous doctor, there follows a very long, fascinating, revelatory self-portrait which looks back to the self-descriptive satiric portraits of the sins in Passus V. It is closer in detailed self-unbuttoning to the techniques of Jean de Meun. The detailed picture of all-pervasive jiggery-pokery which spreads out into every nook and cranny of medieval ordinary life recalls the sinister and uncontrollable clutter of Mr Venus's Anatomy Shop, its preserved dead life oddly illustrative of a loveless, disconnected society. Haukin accumulatively sums up Langland's view of the mercantile life, the commercial pursuit of getting and spending, in the words of recent criticism: 'Practical life, based on and judged by, purely temporal conceptions of goodness.[20] There is nothing mysterious in this, but why, in terms of the structure of the poem, should we have gone to the dinner party in the first place, and why, on the way home, should we have had to experience this garrulous, dishonest, sleight-of-life artist however brilliant as an exposé of medieval Babbittry? The establishment of his manner of living, the methods of his cozenry, his music-hall self-confidence thrust him out beyond aesthetic control: as an artistic creation he comes to belong to 'reality' and so swallows up moral models and philosophical definitions. In so doing, he tends to become a satiric literary end in itself, and therefore unbalances the allegorical plane of the poetic invention. It sinks under his tangible weight. However admirably coherent and morally convincing the antidotes presented by Patience (and they are presented at great length), it is difficult to see Haukin undergoing any major programme of reform. The last view of him (which ends Passus XIV) is of a sorry man, full of the signs of contrition, crying for mercy—but not yet reformed. The sound of his anguish wakes the poet (XIV.332).[21]

Between Passus XIV and XV there is yet another fictional break in continuity. No doubt part of the reason for the length of the poet's waking and the perplexity of his mental and social condition is intended to mark the division between the Dowel Passus and the beginning of the Dobest section (cf. MSS. headings).[22] But the state of foolishness in which the poet falls after waking from the previous dream does not seem to me equatable simply with 'wise folly' or any improvement in his understanding of the life of Dowel. His folly seems to encompass a genuine deficiency, a lack of reasonableness. He admits to a deep alienation from the world and in that alienation a want of moderation, an imbalance in his temperament ('and in that folye I *raved*'). The author says Reason took pity on him and rocked him asleep, as a nurse or mother would do for an upset child. Suddenly, we appear to be back on the highroad to self-discovery, for the creature which the poet encounters is Anima. The face of Anima (who is masculine here and without teeth or mouth) causes the poet to believe that he is the product of black magic and he enquires (like Hamlet) immediately if 'he were Crystes creature'. His soul, in this final manifestation, is no longer the figurative Lady as imagined by his Wit back in Passus IX. This Anima is plainly intended to be a more concentrated, authoritative picture of the poet-figure's mentality, a more systematic and philosophically exact representation. The paradigmatic definition (with strange mistranslation in Latin and English) is a quotation of the Augustinian account in the words of Isidore of Seville. Isidore's verbal formulation (parallelism, partial parallelism, repetition and *polyptoton*) gives the impression of a complete and perfect definition, answering to all criticisms: the soul is a unitary, non-corporeal entity whose nominal multiplicity automatically reflects simple activities carried out in conjunction with the physical operations of the human body. The poet-figure seems to see through the terminological and stylistic symmetry and perfection of this definition, for he jestingly ('al bourdyng that tyme') offers up an analogy based on the various titles bestowed on a bishop ('an hepe'!) Anima must perceive the tone and drift of this deflating argument but Anima quickly agrees to its being 'true' and then savagely rebukes the poet for wishing to know the 'cause' of his names. Further, he is accused of being 'inparfit', though why he should not be, having admitted to being in need of guidance is more than slightly mysterious. Instead, Anima addresses himself to answering Will's supplementary wish to know 'Alle the sciences under þe sonne', by charging that it is both unnatural and unreasonable that any human being (with the exception of Christ) should wish to know everything. But, it must be objected, the poet-dreamer wished to know the answer to one specific philosophical problem. Anima's taking up of the supplementary statement (not a question) is a common form of misrepresentation in order to refute. Here it becomes a universal excuse for refusing to answer Will's justifiable question—and marks a general reluctance to enter into any close philosophical exchanges. Anima's exposition of Romans XII.3 (how far might one seek to know) is basically as anti-intellectual as anything spouted by Dame Study. Further than Isidore's 'definition', Anima is not going to go. Anima has other fish to fry. From the accusation that some friars and university-trained clerks confuse ignorant people and in so doing destroy their religious belief (70) we are moved on to a very long polemic against corrupt clergy. The arboreal imagery of lines 94 ff. leads into Pseudo-Chrysostom in an extremely long Latin quotation. We the reader must be aware by this time that the same process we have experienced before is happening again: the mental power, or representation of self mentality, exists only as a verbal device, as a beginning-motif used to introduce some lengthy form of didactic expression, some form of critical or satiric instruction. The interview with Anima lasts a long time and in its prolonged state consists of a series of detailed criticisms of ecclesiastical practices and malpractices in England and in Europe generally. What is most valuable in Anima's exposition occurs early in the Passus, namely: (1) the emphasis on activity (quoting St Bernard) 'verba vertit in opera'; (2) the definition of Charity (145-189); (3) the emphasis on the necessity of the 'helpe' of Piers (who 'perceives' beyond the actions or words studied by the learned (192, 204): (4) the definition of Piers (205-262), his identification with Christ, and especially his identification with Patience and long-suffering. This constitutes the heart of the positive value of Will's instruction by Anima:

Amonges Cristene men þis myldnesse shulde laste:
In alle manere angres haue þis at herte,
Þat þough þei suffred at þis, god suffred for vs more,
In ensaumple we shulde do so and take ne veniaunce
Of owre foes þat doth vs falsenesse—þat is owre fadres wille.
For wel may euery man wite, if God hadde wolde hymselue,
Sholde neuere Iudas ne iuwe have Ihesus don on rode,
Ne han martired Peter ne Poule, ne in prisoun holden.
Ac he suffred in ensample þat we shulde suffre also,
And seide to suche þat suffre wolde þat *pacientes vincunt*.

                                        (XV. 253-262)
                                        [fol. 65a-65b]

But the medium of this experience of an increase in knowledge is carried out almost exclusively in the didactic and educative mode,
sometimes making use of simple question and answer techniques.
Langland seems to be able to find no other mode, other than the
educative, in which to represent poetically the process of the increase
in self-awareness or the operations of the mind in any of its active or
passive aspects—including (in the 'autobiographical' account of
forty-five misspent years) the activity of memory, and if Professor
Burrow is right, deliberately specified authorial memory. We are de-
prived thereby of specific vividness and the excitement of sharing the
aesthetic recreation of the process of mental experience. Everything
which might be imagined to be interior is externalized and transformed into the didactic as soon as a *rapport* is established between the
poet-figure and his personified mental power. This identity of didactic procedure ensures that all that passes between the poet and his
mentality has a unity of expression and style, but that order of
sameness cannot conceal the fact that the separate functions of the
dreaming poet's mind are not convincingly congruous. When
assembled from the different Passus they do not easily combine into a
whole personality or poetic character or fictional 'mind'. It may be
objected that since the author is at different stages of awareness in the
journey of self-exploration, there is no reason for these faculties to be
capable of being simply combined for the purpose of establishing an
identifiable unity of self. Yet, the discrepancies run deep and this last,
Isidorian, definition of Anima is an exclusive paradigm which admits
little or no adjustment for the mental functions previously personified.

To return to an opening question: can we distinguish between 'thought' and 'expression', is there any significant difference and distance between poet and dreamer? This investigation of the poetic representation of mentality from Passus VIII to Passus XV suggests that the total transformation of 'process' into 'educative expression' makes it almost impossible to distinguish between thought and expression, and that the only distance we can measure lies between what the poet-figure knows and what the mental faculty can further inform him of. The increase in knowledge is not always orderly or clear, for educative augmentation is conducted by sheer accumulation. There are moments of clarity but they are not connected in any aesthetically discernible way with what has gone before. The author as poet or poet-figure does not perform any overt literary act of composition or structural invention to bring this multiplicity of accumulating information into a whole perspective. The process of the poet-figure's experience (in dreams and out of them) is simply left to accumulate. Distinct authorial control and the creation of a sense of the existence of an *archetypus* (in Geoffrey of Vinsauf's literary vocabulary) are not present in the poem—though critics and scholars may labour long to provide the master-plan or missing text, which they may imagine the poem to be a kind of commentary upon.

All this pervasive quality of disconnection, unsustainedness, multiplicity and accumulated didacticism is, I believe, deliberate on Langland's part. For self-knowledge in this 'method' is intended to be beyond the normal processes of acquiring 'knowledge', of finding out. The paradox in Langland's 'theory of knowledge' is that didacticism is the only mode of expression available to the poet, but that the ultimate justification of 'knowing' lies in the individual 'experiencing' (in some unspecified way) of the Incarnation, Passion and Triumph of Christ as presented in Passus XVIII. That process of fused experience and poetic creation provides moral transformation and reformation—but it is restricted to the individual, in this case, the poet-figure. But this last act of 'learning' cannot be acquired vicariously, through literature, through reading the poem. The poem, and the society it is depicting, end in disunity with the poet-figure still searching. Theologically, one supposes, it is as if the Charter of Christ in theory redeems all mankind, but in practice it can only save individual souls who in some sense subscribe their signatures to the Charter, either as beneficiaries or witnesses. It then becomes legally conditional on both parties. How individual souls perform this act of experiencing or subscribing is never explained to us—and given the autonomy of the religious experience, its disconnection from forms of knowing or methods of instruction, it seems incapable of explantion. The traditionists' answer may lie entirely in God's *grace*, the experience cannot be induced, it lies beyond 'mentality'. The *moderni*, the modernists of Langland's century with their absurd doctrine of God's absolute Free Will (a Trinity with and without a *lex Christi*!) would have seen this question as a pseudo-problem. Did Langland manage to subscribe? It might be argued that he subscribed as witness through the poetic act of creating the expression of Passus XVIII—and he had not yet created that Passus when he weakly tried to defend the writing of poetry back in Passus XII. If this conclusion brings us to a position whereby Langland becomes some obscure variety of 'mystic', I think we ought to object to this identification. There is no evidence in the poem that Langland was aware of the paradox or contradiction between 'learning' or 'knowing' and 'religious experience'. Or perhaps we should allow, dogmatically at least, that Langland may have assumed that a reconcilement of these issues was accomplished through the corporate body of Christ, the Church. But this 'formalistic' explanation begs the question of why the poet should engage in such a deeply individual inquisition, such an insatiable and prolonged and inconclusive quest, much less the highly original 'visionary' creative experience of Passus XVIII. Langland was not self-consciously aware of the uniqueness of this experience, and the poem is not only a record of this one significant religious moment or related moments of experience. Frankly, I do not think Langland had understood the nature of his literary and philosophical problem. The detectable presence of an editorial mind or minds in the C-Text may indicate that he had turned the problem of clarification or coherent exposition over to others, even whilst he was alive.

CHAPTER SEVEN

Langland and the Question of Virtual Form

> It looks so like that good old grove
> Where Adam once to Eve made love,
> That any soul alive would swear
> Your trees were educated there.
>
> William Whitehead, *The Answer to An Epistle
> from a Grove in Derbyshire to a Grove in Surrey.*

The conclusion reached by an examination of Langland's representation of 'mentality', the universality of his transformation of all 'images' and poetical experience of cognition into the educative mode, a *stilus didactivus*—and this transformation includes the lexical range of verbs and nouns concerned with mental activity as well as the larger verse units—reopens questions raised in chapters earlier concerning the structural unity of the whole poem. Is it a poem which lacks a controlling *idée*, or is it so much a combining of different poetic and quasi-poetic forms and procedures that as the poem organically grows it becomes progressively more difficult to find an *archetypus* which will accommodate all the diverse elements taken from literary and non-literary areas, a poem which is always outgrowing its vital strength? Or is there some other explanation which may be extracted from the poet's use of didactic transformation as a stylistic and mental principle of growth and organization?

In order to assess my experience of the *narratio* as a continuous reading sensation, a narrative admittedly sustained intermittently and marked by pronounced digressive tendencies, I have had recourse to critical terminology which is modern and unmedieval. The expression 'virtual form', as far as I am aware, has not been applied to the literary questions raised by *Piers Plowman*. Perhaps a short history and definition of the expression will be in order before any experimental application to Langland's poem is attempted. The adjective 'virtual' in combination with nouns such as 'space', 'dream', 'history', and 'form', figures prominently in Professor Susanne K. Langer's absorbing and stimulating book *Feeling and Form* (New York, 1954). Langer, in the context of a discussion of the visual arts remarks (p. 72): 'Like the space 'behind' the surface of a mirror, it is what the physicists call 'virtual space'—an intangible image'. The original use appears to have been limited to optics and is recorded as early as 1834. She identifies the expression 'virtual space' with Adolf Hildebrand's 'perceptual space' (*The Problem of Form in Painting and Sculpture*, New York, 1932). The collocation 'virtual forms' occurs in the chapter summary for pp. 45 ff., though there is no actual usage in the chapter. The germ of the notion can be found earlier on p. 27 in a discussion of musical form:

> The tonal structure we call "music" bears a close logical similarity to the forms of human feeling—forms of growth and attenuation, flowing and stowing, conflict and resolution, speed, arrest, terrific excitement, calm, or subtle activation and dreamy lapses— not joy and sorrow perhaps, but the poignancy of either and both—the greatness and brevity and eternal passing of everything vitally felt. Such is the pattern or logical form, of sentience; and the pattern of music is that same form worked out in pure, measured sound and silence. Music is a tonal analogue of emotive life.

If we were to apply the adjective 'virtual' to the concept of 'tonal analogue', we might say that the 'virtual form' of music is 'emotive life' or 'sentient life'. Further, it might be possible for us to imagine that more specific forms or even genres within the larger traditional demarcations of the arts (music, painting, poetry etc.) may themselves manifest architectonic analogues; they may have 'virtual powers' which derive from some all-pervasive analogous formal coherence. There is no reason why the analogue or 'virtual form' cannot be derived from the primary world of events or activities (such as 'emotion', or 'dream', for example) or from a secondary world of created objects, physical or verbal.

Further along in her study, when she comes to 'poesis', this is exactly what Professor Langer discovers. Pages 230 ff. are concerned to defend the opening passage of Oliver Goldsmith's *The Deserted Village* from Professor Tillyard's charge that the poet is merely creating a 'poetry of direct statement'. This is the passage under discussion:

How often have I loiter'd o'er thy green,
Where humble happiness endear'd each scene!
How often have I paused on every charm,
The shelter'd cot, the cultivated farm,
The never-failing brook, the busy mill,
The decent church that topt the neighb'ring hill;
The hawthorn bush, with seats beneath the shade,
For talking age and whisp'ring lovers made!
How often have I bless'd the coming day
When toil remitting lent its turn to play,
And all the village train, from labour free,
Led up their sports beneath the spreading tree;
While many a pastime circled in the shade,
The young contending as the old survey'd;
And many a gambol frolick'd o'er the ground,
And sleights of art, and feats of strength went round;
And still, as each repeated pleasure tir'd,
Succeeding sports the mirthful band inspir'd.

                                                        (7-24)

In rejecting Tillyard's label of 'poetry of direct statement' which
merely reminds us of other villages like Auburn, Professor Langer
correctly perceives that these lines describing the village green con-
stitute what she calls 'a virtual history', an analogue which is the
primary function of an 'exact and significant form'. The passage
makes up a type of village history, a communal chronicle which links
youth and age, labour and rest, in a common locus where all the activity recalled shares in a circular, recurring pattern which suggests a
rural and seasonal, natural measure of lifetimes—without ever overt-
ly saying so. We perceive this 'history' obliquely not directly ('turn',
'circled', 'went round'). All this 'history' embodies a further
metaphor, what Langer correctly identifies later as 'the Dance of
Life'. But this form of virtual history is not based on any one identifiable written history. Yet what is essentially present in all historical
accounts can be perceived as being recreated by the poet as he seemingly 'objectively' and enumeratively builds up his descriptive
memory of the village of Auburn. The quality of analogousness or
virtualness lies half concealed under the conventional couplet syntax
with its interplay of balanced adjectives, often in pairs, often with in-
terlacing of past and present participial modifiers, deliberate

anaphora ('How often have I ...'), the somewhat commonplace 'democratic' diction akind to that of Shenstone, the sparing use of poeticisms. The deliberate ordinariness, blandness, partially works to conceal the 'virtual form', the analogy which the reader is allowed to discover gradually as the enumeration is prolonged. The 'historical mode' implied and finally embodied in the whole shape and significant function of the central 'green' provides the major source of aesthetic excitement under the deliberately smooth surface; and that excitement is exactly evoked however may times these well-known lines are read.

When we turn to *Piers Plowman* the modern reader will find that the poem makes special claims on his attention and his knowledge. The poem requires a great deal of informed scholarly annotation in two main spheres: (a) that of the fabric of ordinary secular life; and (b) the intricate affiliations between the Vulgate, the liturgy and the patristic and scholarly commentators, in fact, the fabric of ecclesiastic 'learning' and its texts and 'elucidations' (some, including perhaps Langland, would say its 'obfuscations'). But however hard the reader labours to assimilate and 'understand' the poetic use of much of these areas of contextual and historical knowledge, yet the literary and critical inquiry into the question of 'imaginative unity' seems to be little advanced. The poem, however closely and skilfully annotated and explicated, seems to lack a convincing controlling *idée*.[1] Now there may be many reasons for this, including a want of literary or artistic skill and creative intuition on the part of the poet. The ambitious scope of *Piers Plowman* as a fused satiric and religious poem seems to put the overall 'idea' of the poem beyond the application of any single, recognizable Classical, Late Antique or Medieval model. The incorporation of Langland's satiric and religious aims into the *visio* form further limits his possible choice of earlier neo-Classical models. When we survey the range of likely medieval models, we find that no one poem seems to answer to Langland's structural requirements. Dante's *Commedia* answers fairly faithfully to Langland's ambitiousness and massive concentration on contemporary detail, but the intellectual programme of Dante's integration of Classical literary epic (Virgil's *Æneid*) with political and historical ideas and metahistorical patterns[2] is simply outside the range of Langland's reading or learning. It would seem to lie outside Langland's linguistic attainment as well. There is no evidence that he could have read the *Commedia* much less have made sense of its complicated architectonics and highly individual use of imagery and symbols. Equally, there is no evidence to show that Langland consulted any of his contemporary English poets who had successfully written in the dream-vision form, Chaucer and the *Gawain*-poet (if we accept him as the author of *Pearl*). The range of poems which achieves only a limited success in handling the dream-vision form, for example, the *Apocalypsis Goliae* in Latin, the *Tournoiement de l'Antichrist* in Old French and the *Wynner and Wastour* and *Parliament of the Thre Ages* in Middle English, Langland may have read either in part or *in toto*: quotations and verbal reminiscences can be traced. But none of these poems possesses the architectonic power individually or collectively to provide the author of *Piers Plowman* with a central, controlling Idea. None of the satiric poems from Juvenal to the medieval Latin imitations from the twelfth century onwards would have been of much help in providing coherence or formal organization: the *farrago* principle is too much in evidence. Besides, the *satura* form largely neglects the positive religious and theological programme of Langland's poem, even where the medieval *satura* founded its display of criticism on a Christian or ecclesiastical point of view. The only single poem which approaches the satiric energy and digressive augmentation of *Piers Plowman* is Jean de Meun's continuation of the *Roman*. Again, Jean's concept of the structure of the *Roman* is too lacking in a sustained narrative rhythm to have been much use as an 'idea' for Langland's work of art.[3] Jean's *Roman* also lacks positivity of religious spirit, the undermining and subversive effect of Jean's satiric *esprit* shows itself dominant in nearly every inventive aspect of the poem.[4] Langland's handling of the dream material is not especially dream-like in its method of presentation, either of actual dream or of the literary formulation of dream as found in Chaucer, Machaut, Froissart or the *Pearl*. Inconsequentiality and suddenness of transitions arise less from an intention to create dream plasticity than it more easily derives from the narrative transitions and digressiveness of the long satiric and didactic narrative inventions of the Middle Ages, whether they are nominally *visiones* or not. In the last analysis Langland does not seem to have been interested in literary inventions or models, and, consequently, it is extremely difficult to see *Piers Plowman* as a normative medieval 'form' which can be derived from, or related to, any one pre-existing model.

If we can accept this conclusion about the 'idea' of the poem and the difficulty of locating a convincing model for Langland's inventive capacity, we are still faced with the possibility that the poet, in finding

himself left with the alternative of combining a number of forms or
genres, arrived at the necessity of creating a verbal amalgam which
effectively prevented the artist from realising a unity of formal design.
A synthesis of the visional, the satiric, moral and didactic narratives
would require a formidable grasp of literary architectonics, a perception of effective unifying force well beyond Langland's ability. But
this explanation fails to account for a special and unique quality in
Piers Plowman, a special and energetic quality which is not the result of
the combining of forms or poetic synthesizing of any kind; nor can it
be explained as the simple result of a strong social or religious conviction. It does not arise, either, out of the lyric-poetic intensity of the
writer's response to Christ's Incarnation and Passion—although this
impulse creates in Passus XVIII a coherence of poetic elements un-
paralled elsewhere in the poem over such a sustained and complete
narrative unit. This special quality which seems to be present in all
the Passus is an underlying authorial yearning, an intellectual appetite for the achievement of a complete understanding or perhaps a
realisation of an *ars vivendi Christiana*. This insatiable appetite seems to
me to have little to do with the salvation of one's soul, and more to do
with the individual and corporate maintaining of a Christian society
and nation. I can well see Langland agreeing with Robert Holcot's
moral emphasis as enunciated in *Lectio* 120: '... nullam tamen ivit
sine labore.'; and the neo-Stoic work-ethic quoted from Boethius, *De
Consolatione* IV. m. 7 (this is all taken from Seneca): 'ubi inducit
exemplum trium vivorum illustrium, qui labores maximos pro virtute
et gloria temporali sustinuerunt, videlicet Agamemnonis, Ulyxis et
Herculeis'.[5] In Langland's yearning for the perfection to be found in
such a state of understanding, he naturally approaches near to the
perfecting impulse which lies at the heart of Dante's great poem. It
justified Professor Bennett in his early wireless broadcast 'William
Langland's World of Visions' (reprinted in the *Listener*, 2 March,
1950) linking the two poets together in terms of intellectual commitment. It is this same force in Langland which *facit versus*, and it creates
the endless muddles as well as the moments of intellectual clarification
in its unsatisfied and perhaps insatiable quest for completeness of
knowledge. Muddle and clarification are integral parts of the
Langlandian dialectic, one seems to depend on the other. Anima
severely rebukes the poet for his pride and presumption at wanting to
know *completely*. All of Langland's mental faculties are a cheerless,
debunking, rebuking collection. The discouraging, cheerless aspect of

them constitutes the only argument for a continuous mental congruity between them, from Thought to Anima, a common temperament.

A curious fact is that, although this insatiable intellectual appetite for the wholeness or completeness of practical moral knowledge is an active, an hyper-active, force in the poet Langland, its activity in the poet-figure Will creates a certain radical passivity, a receptiveness in the narrator to be taught, educated, instructed in this *ars vivendi Christiana*, this applied version of the *lex Christi*. The poet-figure may, on occasion, argue or put up a brief intellectual struggle, but normally he very quickly acquiesces and so achieves a state of receptivity, a receptiveness for being educated towards a better or more complete understanding. The purpose of this pacific dialectic is to create a dialogue between the active and passive aspects of educative experience. In this way, the poet-figure and his 'mentality' create an educational situation where there is a giving and receiving of information. This process of dialogue, of course, extends beyond the personifications of Will's mental powers to embrace all other encounters with personifications and 'characters' which have been created for inclusion in the poem.

It follows, then, that there would appear to be a connection between the surface level of style, the *stylus didactivus*, and the deeper, more significant use of educative dialogue between the poet-figure and all the inventions of his creative mind, all the dramatic personifications of the poem. It is here, at this point, that I should like to introduce Professor Langer's modern terminology, 'virtual form', into my discussion of *Piers Plowman*. Putting aside all editorial apparatus and reading the poem in the B-Text version straight through in MS. Laud Misc. 581, what is my sensation as a reader of the rhythmic units and chief attributes of the *narratio*, the narrative experienced as one whole sweeping movement, from the Prologue to Passus XX? Surprisingly, it turns out that the poem becomes much shorter, more compact. It only occupies three reading sessions of two hours each, and, inspite of the longeurs of Passus X-XV, the attributes of the narrative seem to me strong and unmistakable. Each Passus, no matter how individually structured, comes to lose its *differentia*, certain contours are not retained by the memory whilst certain other features gradually become more memorable: a continuousness of sequence moving from one Passus to another emerges. This progressive sequence is composed of a series of dominant recurring rhythms: augmentation, repetition, summarization, anticipation, and above all, recapitulation, repetitions which invariably lead to an ever widening complexity of augmentation again. There is a sense in which the process using these vital rhythms becomes, from a logical point of view, 'thematic'. Intellectually, from our accumulation of content and meaning, we tend therefore to see, or are tempted to see, the structure of the poem as thematic, whereas it is not. The distinguishing characteristic of the *narratio* cannot be expressed simply by this term: the so-called 'themes' only make up a small part of this matrix of rhythms: the narrative matrix is larger and more inclusive than 'thematicism'.

If I were to adopt Professor Langer's expression, 'virtual form', what collectively do these rhythms remind me of? They remind me of the learning process itself, especially the old-fashioned grammatical method of teaching and learning the Latin language or Greek language, where augmentation and accumulation is accompanied by themes, repetition, recapitulation and summarization; reiteration, the constant addition of new elements, then a rehearsal of the older material incorporating the new, the use of thematic return. The related elements of didacticism in the poem are given the dominant form or mode of learning itself. The virtual form of Langland's poem is that of the learning process, the active and passive educative mode in its traditional grammarian's form. It was no accident, then, that one strong thematic unit (Dowel, Dobet, Dobest) was originally conceived as a grammatical metaphor.[6] The recurring citation of the *Disticha Catonis* is no accident either, for that text belongs to the basic medieval curriculum of the learning of the Latin language, as well as the acquisition of moral precepts. The virtual form or mode of the poem arises out of Langland's personal experience of a medieval basic education, and his natural, instinctive affection for the experience of grammatical learning. There are several passages in which he comments on this experience of 'lore' and 'love'. The most important testimony is that contained in the C-Text, VI, lines 35 ff.:

'Whanne ich ʒong was', quath ich, 'meny ʒer hennes,
My fader and my frendes founden me to scole,
Tyl ich wist wyterliche what holy writ menede
And what is best for the body as the bok telleth,
And sykerest for the soule by so ich wolle continue.
And ʒut fond ich neuere, in faith, sytthen my frendes deyden,
Lyf that me lyked bote in thes longe clothes.'

This is a quiet, convincing witness to the abiding impression made on Langland by his early education. In spite of the Everyman editor's temptation to render 'scole' by 'university', I think Langland here means 'school', the basic, very pre-university education, interrupted and ended by the death of his relatives (ME 'frendes') who were his sponsors. A deeply, instinctive yearning for this educative life is experienced 'virtually' in the active creating of the poem. It is a form of surrogate activity rooted in the personality of the writer. But I believe what is recreated by the virtual mode of the poem is an abstraction, a generalised or 'essentialised' educative life. The poet has no intention of referring the reader to any single grammar or educational primer. It is like the 'virtual history' of Goldsmith's *The Deserted Village*. Therefore, there is no logical or specific verbal model. Medieval grammars regularly made use of a variety of teaching techniques which may be found reflected in *Piers Plowman*: the use of fable, dialogue, proverbs and riddles, for example.[7] But the generalised modal architectonic is the essential component in the poet's use of virtual form. The poem's uniqueness lies in the width and breadth of its 'virtual power'. The closest analogue I would suggest is that the major division of *Piers Plowman* into prologue -Passus VII; Passus VIII-XX, may be a distant memory of the division of Donatus's widely-used grammar (mentioned in Passus V. 209, possibly in an abridged form) into two parts, the *Ars Minor* (short and fundamental) and the *Ars Major* (longer and more complicated). Beyond that 'memory' I would not care to go.

In the process of trying to put into words the application of Langer's 'virtual' to 'Langland's *Piers Plowman*, I find that I have begun to waver between 'form' and 'mode'. In the last analysis, I think that perhaps 'mode' is the clearer and less ambiguous term. Langland subconsciously creates for the poem an educative mode, a *modus didactivus*, and that all-pervasive rhythm cannot act as an organizing factor on the reader's consciousness. It cannot be elevated into a verbal 'form'. It is not an adequate substitute for the 'idea' or *archetypus*. The 'virtual mode' can be extracted from the poem, but once extracted and identified it cannot be made to contribute to the unity of the poem any more than one could convincingly argue that the unity of Spenser's *Faerie Queene* is *Farielond*. C. S. Lewis's original observation in the *Allegory of Love* still holds true: 'He is confused and monotonous, and hardly makes his poetry into a poem.'[8]

NOTES

CHAPTER ONE

[1] Cf. F. Hartt, *Giulio Romano*, 2 vols, Yale (1958). Vol.i., p. 107-8, p. 114; vol.ii., figs. 38, 40, 41, 180-186.

[2] J. D. Mackie, *The Earlier Tudors 1485-1558*, Oxford (1952), pp. 1-2.

[3] *The Arte of English Poesie by George Puttenham*, ed. G. D. Willcock and A. Walker, Cambridge (1936), p. 62.

[4] Cf. R. Tuve, *Allegorical Imagery*, Princeton (1966), p. 264n.

[5] J. Lawlor, 'The Imaginative Unity of *Piers Plowman*', *RES* ns 8 (1957), pp. 113-126.

[6] R. Woolf, 'Some Un-medieval Qualities of *Piers Plowman*' *EC* 12 (1962), pp. 111-125.

[7] D. Mills, 'The Role of the Dreamer in *Piers Plowman*' in *Piers Plowman: Critical Approaches*, ed. S. S. Hussey, London (1969), pp. 180-212.

CHAPTER TWO

[1] H. Meroney, 'The Life and Death of Longe Wille', *ELH* 17 (1950).

[2] E. Rickert, 'John But: Messenger and maker', *MP* 11 (1913-14), pp. 107-16. Cf. Bodley MS. Rawlinson poet. 137, fol. 41b. There is evidence in the *Cal. of Close Rolls* for 5 November, 1379, of a grant of income from the king to John But, 'one of the king's messengers'. This would accord well with But's concern for Richard ('first to rekne Richard. kyng of þis rewme/And alle lordis þat louyn him . lely in herte ...'). These lines are followed by a note of the scribe's name ('Nomen scriptoris. tilot plenus amoris'). Kane's note is mistaken here. 'Tilot' is the scribe's surname, as any standard work on English surnames would have confirmed. The Latin phrase 'plenus amoris' is a common tag used exclusively by scribes to accompany a signing of the text. Kane's statement about early ownership is not accurate. A young man's signature (early sixteenth century) appears on fol. 24a: 'Richard Barnard'.

[3] Cf. Talbot Donaldson, *Piers Plowman: the C-Text and its Poet* (New Haven and London, 1949) pp. 18 ff.

[4] Cf. D. C. Fowler, 'A New Edition of the B-Text of *Piers Plowman*', *Yearbook of English Studies* 7 (1977), pp. 23-42.

[5] J. A. W. Bennett, *Chaucer at Oxford and at Cambridge* Oxford (1974) p. 32.

[6] But cf. Schmidt, *The Vision of Piers Plowman* (Everyman, London, 1978), p. xii: 'There is no way of going back to Skeat and no point in reproducing his text as the original work of the poet or any approaching it.' But he has admitted on the same page that there is no uncorrupt archetype. His own Everyman text must be as dependent on Kane and Donaldson as it is on the manuscript on which he claims to have based his text (Trinity College, Cambridge, B.15.17).

[7] Kane and Donaldson's extremely condensed sections on the palaeographical descriptions of the MSS are generally inadequate and honeycombed with a variety of

errors, at least as far as the Bodleian Library's holdings of manuscripts which I have checked.

⁸ Cf. Gilbert Highet, *The Poet Juvenal*, Oxford (1954) *passim*, on poetic unifying devices.

⁹ J. Norton-Smith, *Geoffrey Chaucer* (London, 1974), pp. 211-225.

CHAPTER THREE

¹ Earlier eighteenth-century inquiries into medieval form and style are not marked by the same attention to scientific exactitude. The Victorians were better equipped as scholars of the medieval period. Cf. Kenneth Clark, *The Gothic Revival*, London (1950), *passim*. The reference to William Whewell in Parker's quotation is to *Architectural Notes on German Churches*, Cambridge (1842).

² Cf. P. Gradon, *Form and Style in Early English Literature*, London (1971), pp. 84 ff.; A. V. C. Schmidt (ed.), *The Vision of Piers Plowman*, London (1978), pp. xxv-xxxiv; E. Salter, 'Medieval Poetry and the Figural View of Reality', *PBA* LIV (1968), pp. 73-92.

³ *A Land*, New York (1952), p. 197.

⁴ C. S. Lewis, *The Discarded Image*, Cambridge (1964), pp. 199-223.

⁵ H. S. Bennett, *Chaucer and the Fifteenth Century*, Oxford (1947), p. 15. The italics are mine.

⁶ J. A. W. Bennett, *The Parlement of Foules*, Oxford (1957), p. 51.

⁷ Schmidt, *op. cit.*, p. xx. He seems to wish to avoid saying that the poem is divided in this way, but is nevertheless obliged to retain the term 'epilogue'.

⁸ The noun 'Imaginatyf' in Langland almost certainly begins by signifying the activity of the mind which forms and retains images supplied by the external 'wits' or senses but has the additional capacity of forming images of the past and future. But, as always in Langland, it develops quickly additional powers, especially an obsession with final 'salvation' and a penchant for censorious warnings. The dramatizing power of the poet's creative imagination which renders 'Ymaginatyf' as a tedious old family retainer gets in the way of philosophical exactitude.

⁹ Cf. T. F. S. Turville-Petre, *A Study of the Parlement of the Thre Ages*, Oxford unpublished B.Litt. thesis, d. 1690, pp. 19 ff.

¹⁰ See the observations on rhythm in T. Turville-Petre, *The Alliterative Revival*, Cambridge (1977), p. 60, and Emrys Jones's remarks in *Henry Howard, Earl of Surrey: Poems*, Oxford (1964), p. 134.

¹¹ 'Phraseological' is elevated to a primary stylistic attribute by Professor John Lawlor in his *Piers Plowman: an Essay in Criticism*, London (1962).

¹² Cf. E. R. Curtius, *European Literature and the Latin Middle Ages*, London (1953), pp. 242-3.

¹³ In Bodley MS. Laud Misc. 581 (fol. 4b) a sixteenth-century hand has written 'the rounings of the dongen'. This probably refers to the cursing of one's being born. Compare Arcite's words in the *Knight's Tale* 1223-4:

> He seyde: 'Allas that day I was born,
> Now is my prison worse than biforn.'

¹⁴ *Opera Minora*, ed. J. Loserth (1913), p. 40.

¹⁵ F. P. Pickering, *The Anglo-Norman Text of the Holkham Bible Picture Book*, Anglo-Norman Texts, vol. xxiii Oxford (1971), pp. xix-xx.

[16] M. Hanna, *The Treatment of the Passion in the B-Text of Piers Plowman*, Oxford unpublished B.Litt. thesis, d. 688, (1954), *passim*. This study is indispensible for an understanding of Langland's poetic methods.

[17] Cf. J. Norton-Smith, *Geoffrey Chaucer*, London (1974), pp. 62-72 for an account of the function of irony in the Prologue.

[18] From MS. *Ca.*, printed in Langlois's Notes, vol. iii, pp. 313-4, 11s. 55-66, especially 57[20]-58[30].

[19] The expression derives from Mme. Odette de Mourgues' study on La Fontaine. Cf. Professor Gray's convincing explication of Henryson's *Fables* in *Robert Henryson*, Leiden (1980), pp. 61 ff. and pp. 73-4.

[20] The four-fold allegorists or Pseudo-Can Grandites were completely exploded by R. S. Crane, 'On Hypotheses in "Historical Criticism"': Apropos of Certain Contemporary Medievalists', in his *The Idea of the Humanities and Other Essays Critical and Historical* II, Chicago (1967), pp. 236-60.

[21] Cf. The York Medieval Texts' Introduction to Langland selections (*Piers Plowman*) ed. E. Salter and D. Pearsall, London (1967). Much of the introduction is useful and informative, but the 'method' can be used to prove anything about Langland's theory of communication.

[22] Sister Marie Brisson, 'The Influence of Frère Laurent's *La Somme le Roi* on Frère Robert's *Le Chastel Perilleux*', *MÆ* 36 (1967), pp. 134 ff.

[23] M. Hanna, *op. cit.*, pp. 99 and 114. But some of the imagery had already been appropriated and used by poets, cf. *Le Tournoiement d'Enfer*, written *c.* 1285, ed. A. Längfors, *Romania* 44, pp. 511-558, especially lines 1752 ff. on virginity:

> Li escuz fut cortais et biaus
> Si i fut painz saint Gabriaus
> Qui la novele li aporte.
> Par Eve fut close la porte
> De Paradiz, mès desfermee
> Fut par ceste beneüree
> Dont je vous ai tenu parole.

[24] *Ibid.*, pp. 41 ff. an author known to Langland.

[25] Cf. Skeat's Index to vol. ii. p. 480, for the frequent use of parable.

[26] See B. J. Whiting and H. E. Whiting, *Proverbs, Sentences, and Proverbial Phrases from English Writings Mainly Before 1500* (Cambridge, Mass., and London, 1969), N64, D80, H204. In each case, Langland is the first recorded example.

[27] *Op. Cit.*, pp. 13-15.

[28] Curtius, *op. cit.*, p. 119, 414 ff.

[29] C-Text, Passus IV. 292-415. This passage has provoked modern comments, cf. A. V. C. Schmidt, 'Two Notes on *Piers Plowman*', *N. & Q.* n.s.16 (1969), pp. 285-6. M. N. K. Mander 'Grammatical Analogy in Langland and Alan of Lille', *N & Q.* n.s.26 (1979), pp. 501-504; A. V. C. Schmidt, 'Langland's Pen/Parchment Analogy in *Piers Plowman*, B1X, 38-40', *N. & Q.* n.s.27 (1980), pp. 538-9.

[30] *Notes on the Pilgrim's Progress*.

[31] Curtius, *op. cit.*, p. 71, p. 501.

[32] *William Dunbar*, Leiden (1981), p. 105.

CHAPTER FOUR

[1] *Institutio Oratoria* X. i. 93-96.

[2] *Etymologiae* VIII. vii. 'De Poetis'.

[3] Cf. F. J. E. Raby, *A History of Secular Latin Poetry*, Oxford (1957), vol. ii. pp. 89-102; 190-227.

[4] Cf. P. Lehmann, *Die Parodie im Mittelalter*, Munich (1922), pp. 85 ff.

[5] R. M. Durling, *The Figure of the Poet in Renaissance Epic*, Harvard (1965), pp. 25-6.

[6] A possible exception is S. T. Knight's 'Satire in *Piers Plowman*' in *Piers Plowman: Critical Approaches*, ed. S. S. Hussey, London (1969), pp. 279-309.

[7] Except for the sidedishes there was a wondrous fritter composed entirely of vices, all cooked unnaturally and plastered all over with a sauce from Chartres.

[8] But cf. S. T. Knight., *op. cit.*, 'Langland has expanded the nature of satire'.

[9] ed. Méon, *Fabliaux et Contes*, Paris (1808), vol. ii., pp. 276-286.

[10] J. Stowe, *A Survey of London*, 1598, p. 82.

[11] Cf. *Roman de la Rose*, lines 11181 ff.

[12] This signifies a dereliction of duty. Part of the phraseology is used of a skulking, unhelpful 'Clergie' in the A-Text XII. 35: 'Clergie into a caban crepte anon after/And drow the dore after him ...'

[13] The list of names and surnames in lines 315 ff. contains names which do not alliterate. This perhaps indicates that some names may have been traditional and some just invented for the nonce.

[14] Invidia's green pallor perhaps may be traced ultimately back to Ovid's figure of Palor in *Metamorphoses* II. 775 ff. via the *Roman's* account of Avarice (199 ff.): 'Et ausi vert come une cive' which Chaucer translates: 'And also grene as any leek'.

[15] John Stowe, *A Survey of London*, 1598, p. 71.

[16] M. C. Spalding, *The Middle English Charters of Christ*, Bryn Mawr College Monographs, vol. 15 (1914).

[17] R. Woolf, 'The Tearing of the Pardon', in *Piers Plowman: Critical Approaches*, ed. S. S. Hussey, London (1969), pp. 50-75.

[18] The expression 'pies hele' and the compound (A and C Texts) 'pie-hele' is an ″απαξ λεγ. The nouns occur separately in ME but there is no convincing parallel I can remember. The accepted explanation rests on later usage where 'heel' figuratively comes to mean a 'crust' or 'end' of bread. Mr Edward Wilson draws my attention to an instance of a phrase in ME 'not worth a pie', recorded by Whiting (*op. cit*) p. 177. The phrase comes from the fourteenth-century poem *Duke Rowlande*, 1. 1157. (ed. S. J. Herrtage, *E.E.T.S.* 35 (1880), p. 91): 'зour lawes are noghte worthe a pye.' The O.F. original reads 'ne valent une alie'. Presumably this is the noun *alie*, a 'service-apple', recorded in the *Roman* 1352, which Chaucer renders 'aleyes'. Unfortunately, the French shows no immediate light on the ME equivalent noun.

CHAPTER FIVE

[1] Gillian Evans, 'Insight in the Thought of St Anselm', *Reading Medieval Studies*, Vol. i (1975), pp. 1-15.

[2] M. C. Spalding, *The Middle English Charters of Christ*, Bryn Mawr College Monographs, vol. 15 (1914).

[3] Dame Juliana Berners, *Boke of Cote-Armure* in the *Boke of St. Albans*, 1486 (sig. aii).

⁴ Cf. M. Hanna, *Op. Cit.*, p. 24 ff.

⁵ Peter Dronke ('Arber Caritatis', in *Medieval Studies for J. A. W. Bennett*, Oxford (1981), pp. 207-253, calls our attention to the origin of the tree of charity in Augustine's commentary on the first Epistle of John (seemingly unnoticed by Langland scholars) (p. 214). But he might have quoted the more extensive allegorical passage in Augustine's *Liber de Verbis Domini Salvatoris* (in Evangelio secundum Matthæum), Sermo XII, where the *arber charitatis* has 'circumfessio arboris est humilitas poenitentis' and 'cophinum stercoris, sordes poenitentiæ'.

⁶ *Op. cit.*, p. 145. But see P. Dronke, *cap. cit.*, pp. 207-253, where Langland's use of the 'tree of charity' is seen as a typical example of the 'disorder of the allegorical scenery' (German in origin) and that Langland's choice of arboreal *topos* automatically commits him to 'disordered scenery'. Cf. p. 213: 'Moreover, as I hope to indicate, the most memorable allegorical trees had always been presented with the help of disordered scenery.' This topos-dominated theory abandons the question of authorial intention or specific æsthetic necessity.

⁷ Attempts to emend *lone* to *loue* (palaeographically possible) would create more serious problems in this context. Compare B-Text, XI. 48: (of Fortune's activity at the start of a dream): 'And into þe londe of Longynge, *allone* she me brouȝte.' This is supported by the dream context of *The Kingis Quair* 531. The solitary emphasis may be a memory of Daniel 10.8: 'Ego autem relictus solus vidi visionem grandem hanc ...'.

⁸ This echoes the imagery of Passus VIII, 94-5, where Dobest carries a bishop's crozier hooked at one end to haul 'men' from hell. The other end is piked to 'pulte adoun the wikked'.

⁹ Cf. J. Ruskin, *Modern Painters*, Part IV. Chap. Viii, sect. 4 (London, 1892, vol. iii, p. 99): 'A fine grotesque is the expression in a moment, by a series of symbols thrown together in bold and fearless connections, of truths which it would have taken a long time to express in any verbal way, and of which the connection is left for the beholder to work out for himself.'

¹⁰ This psalmic passage (and interpretation) perhaps lies behind the cryptic phrase in Passus V. 500-1: 'meletyme of seyntes', though the 'seyntes' probably include the souls of the virtuous in Limbo as well as *multa corpora sanctorum* not so specified. Cf. Professor Bennett's note, *op. cit.*, p. 185.

¹¹ Cf. J. Ruskin, *Modern painters*, part III, sect. 1, chap. IV, para. 10.

¹² The compound 'mynut-whil' occurs first in Passus XI. 273. The compound seems to be restricted to Langland in ME.

¹³ The 'two brode eyen' of 'Book' (228) probably represents the Old and New Testaments with their Prophets and Evangelists. Isidore, *Etymologiae VI* in his discussion of the Evangelists dwells on the passage in Revelations 4.6: 'four beasts full of eyes', remarking 'Nam et oculis plena erant intus et foris, quoniam praevidentur ea Evangelia quae dicta sunt a prophetis, et quae promiserant in priori tempore.' The tendency to pair and contrast (intus et foris; Evengelia/prophetis; praevidentur/promiserant) connects with *plena oculis*. Some details here have been taken from Augustine's commentary on Revelations 4.6.

¹⁴ A/209/17.

¹⁵ The imagery and poetic motifs descend ultimately from Prudentius's *Cathemerinon* I, given wide currency by the Lauds hymn 'Ales diei nuncius'. There is a late ME translation of the hymn in B.L.MS. Add. 24193. Cf. D. Gray, *A Selection of Religious Lyrics*, Oxford (1975), no. 75.

¹⁶ F. P. Pickering, *Art and Literature in the Middle Ages*, London (1970), p. 160 and plate 11a.

[17] In many manuscripts the title of the poem contains the expression 'Petrus Plowman'. 'There are two names in balance, one scriptural, Latin and hieratic, the other solidly human, functional and English', as Professor Bennett reminded us long ago.

[18] There is an OF equivalent noun in use by 1350. ME does not find 'longanimity' until the mid fifteenth century.

CHAPTER SIX

[1] *art. cit.*, p. 205.

[2] Professor Bennett (*Gower Selections*, p. 173) was inclined to credit the four line 'epistola' (really an epigram) on Gower ('Quam cinxere freta') to Strode and also the commendatory lines (in elegiac couplets) attached to the *Vox Clamantis*. I think the 'Eneados Bucolis' (Macaulay, vol. iv, p. 361) written by 'quidam Philosophus' should be attributed to Strode. The combination of the very restricted leonine riming with the variation and interlocking of syntax within the classical chiastic pattern of the distich form is extremely skilfull. But these small poems, if genuine Strode, tell us nothing of his larger poetic interests.

[3] Cf. A. B. Emden, *A biographical Register of the University of Oxford to 1500*, vol. i. (1958), p. 297.

[4] J. A. Weisheipl, *Early Fourteenth-Century Physics of the 'Merton School'*, Oxford D.Phil. thesis d.1776 (1956).

[5] Adam: *Morte et Vita, Sompno.*

Adam de Bockfeld: *Sensu et sensato, Somno et vigilia, Anima.*

Adam de Bouchemefort: *Anima, Memoria et reminiscentia.*

Alanus: *Anima.*

Aquinas, Thomas: *Anima, Memoria et reminiscentia, Sensu et Sensato.*

Arnoldus de Villanova: *Confortatio memoriae, Interpretatio de visionibus in somnis.*

Augustine: *Anima et spiritu, De quantitate animae.*

Averroes: *Anima, Intellectu, Memoria et reminiscentia, Sensu et sensato, Sompno et vigilia, Somno.*

Avicenna: *Actionibus et passionibus, Anima, Intellectu, Sompno et vigilia.*

Bacon, Roger (?): *Somno et vigilia.*

Baconthorpe, John: *Anima, Somno et vigilia, Potentiis animae.*

Bartholomaeus de Brugis: *Sensu agente.*

Bernard: *Spiritu et anima.*

Blasius of Parma: *Anima.*

Buridan, John: *Anima, Memoria et reminiscentia, Sensu et sensato, Somno et vigilia.*

Burley, Walter: *Anima, Sensu et sensato, Somno et vigilia, Sensibus, Tractatus de quinque sensibus.*

Caelius, Aurelianus: *Acutis passionibus, Diaeticis passionibus.*

Duns Scotus: *Anima, Sensu et sensato.*

Grosseteste, Robert: *Anima.*

Guido Terrenus: *Anima.*

Gundissalinus, Dominicus: *Anima.*

Henricus de Oyta: *Anima.*

Heytesbury, William: *Sensu composito.*

Jacobus de Alexandria: *Anima, Memoria est reminiscentia, Sensu et sensato, Somno et vigilia.*

Jacobus de Duaco: *Anima, Sompno et vigilia.*
Jacobus Lombardus: *Anima.*
Jean de Jandun: *Anima, Memoria et reminiscentia, Sensu et sensato, Somno et vigilia.*
Lambertus de Monte: *Anima.*
Matthew of Aquasparta: *Anima.*
Michael Scot: *Anima.*
Oresme, N.: *Anima.*
Paul of Venice: *Anima.*
Peckham, John: *Anima* (cf. Emden, vol. iii, pp. 1445-7).
Petrus de Alvernia: *Anima, Memoria et reminiscentia, Sensu et sensato, Sompno et vigilia.*
Petrus Hispanus: *Anima.*
Renham, Henry: *Anima, Somno et vigilia* (cf. Emden, vol. iii. p. 1565).
Siger of Brabant: *Anima intellectiva, Anima, Somno et vigilia.*
Simon of Faversham: Aristotelian commentaries (cf. Emden, ii. p. 672).
Thomas de Willetonia: *Anima* (? = Thomas de Wylton, Fellow of Merton).
William of Auvergne: *Anima.*
William Hothum: *Anima* (cf. Emden, ii. 970-1).
William de Moerbeck: *Anima.*
William de St. Thierry: *Natura corporis et animae, Physica animae.*
John de Mechlinia: *Sensu et sensato, Somno et vigilia.*
John of Rupella: *Anima.*
John Versor, *Anima. Memoria et reminiscentia, Sensu et sensato, Somno et vigilia.*
Kilwardby, Robert: *Anima facultatibus.* But cf. Emden, *op. cit.*, p. 1502. This work
   should be ascribed to Geoffrey Aspale? Kilwardby was an Anti-Aristotelian? For
   Aspale, cf. Emden, vol. i., pp. 60-61. He also wrote a commentary to the *Sensu
   et sensato.* But cf. Neil Ker, 'The Books of Philosophy Distributed at Merton
   College in 1372 and 1375' in *Medieval Studies for J. A. W. Bennett*, Oxford (1981),
   pp. 347-394. Dr. Ker accepts Kilwardby as the author of a commentary on
   Aristotle's *Prior Analytics* (p. 372). One should also consult the excellent
   unpublished Oxford D.Phil. thesis by P. O. Lewry, *Robert Kilwardby's
   Writings on the Logica Vetus studied with regard to their teaching and method*, Oxford
   D.Phil. (1978).

[6] J. Norton-Smith, *Geoffrey Chaucer*, London (1974), pp. 88 ff.

[7] H. C. Mainzer, *A Study of the sources of the Confessio Amantis of John Gower*, Oxford
D.Phil. thesis (1967), D.Phil. d. 4209.

[8] Julia Winterbotham, *John Gower's use of Ovid in the Confessio Amantis*, Reading
University M.A. thesis (1978).

[9] Cf. M. A. Manzalaoui, " 'Noght in the Register of Venus'. Gower's English
Mirror for Princes" in *Medieval Studies for J. A. W. Bennett*, Oxford (1981), pp. 160-183
for a full discussion of Gower's use of sources in Book VII of the *Confessio Amantis.*

[10] Cf. J. A. W. Bennett, 'Nosce te ipsum: Some Medieval Interpretations', *J. R. R.
Tolkien, Scholar and Storyteller: Essays in Memoriam*, ed. M. Salu and R. T. Farrell (Ithaca
and London, 1979), pp. 138-158.

[11] Cf. J. Norton-Smith, *Review of The Shorter Poems of Gavin Douglas*, ed. by Priscilla
Bawcutt, *MÆ* XXXVII, (1968), p. 353-357.

[12] J. Norton-Smith, *Bodleian MS. Fairfax 16*, Scolar Press, London (1979), p. xxv-
xxvi.

[13] But cf. Schmidt, *op. cit.*, 327 who accepts that there is a progression towards
'knowledge' (*OED.* Wit. 11).

[14] The suggestion made by Mr Goodridge is rejected by Schmidt, *op. cit.*, p. 327. The suggestion was originally made by Professor J. A. W. Bennett.

[15] T. Halpern (ed.), 'Cassiodous's *De anima*', *Traditio* (1960), pp. 19-109. The other powers are: (3) principal (meditative); (4) vital (bodily warmth); (5) detectative (desire).

[16] Cf. Schmidt's note, *op. cit.*, 331. But cf. J. Coleman, *Piers Plowman and the Moderni*, Rome (1981) *passim* for an entirely different analysis of the fourteenth-century debates in theology. She sees Langland as substantially in agreement with the 'modernists'. I think she incidentally proves that Langland had more in common with Wycliff (see, pp. 74 ff.). For a wholly sceptical view of the specific influence of Wycliff's writings on Langland, see P. Gradon, 'Langland and the Ideology of Dissent', *PBA* LXVI (1980), London, 1982, pp. 179-205.

[17] Cf. J. A. Burrow, '*Langland Nel mezzo Del Camin*', in *Medieval Studies for J. A. W. Bennett*, Oxford (1981), pp. 21-41.

[18] J. Coleman, *op. cit.*, pp. 108-146. She seems to be convinced that Langland understood the contemporary hair-splitting of the *moderni*.

[19] J. A. Burrow, *art. cit.*, pp. 22-24.

[20] Cf. Schmidt's note, *op. cit.*, p. 341, quoting Maguire.

[21] But cf. J. A. Alford, 'Haukyn's Coat: Some Observations on *Piers Plowman* B.XV. 22-7', *MÆ* XLIII (1974), pp. 133-8.

[22] The physical *dispositio* of the *vita* section presents no real problem. Passus VIII-XX is roughly twice as long as the *visio* (2,990 lines) which takes about two hours reading time (for this unit as a 'norm', cf. *Geoffrey Chaucer*, London (1974), pp. 90 ff.). The *visio* is subdivided into two main sections (Prol.-IV; V-VII) which correspond to the main dreams. The *vita* (*c.* 4,897 lines) is divided into two roughly equal units (VIII-XIV, 2,333 lines: XV-XX, 2,544 lines), the major division occurring between the lives of Dowel and Dobet (XIV/XV). This unit subdivides into Dowel (VIII-XIV), Dobet (XV-XVIII), Dobest (XIX-XX).

CHAPTER SEVEN

[1] But see R. E. Kaske, 'Holy Church's Speech and the Structure of *Piers Plowman*' in *Chaucer and Middle English Studies in Honour of Rossell Hope Robbins*, ed. B. Rowland, London (1974), pp. 320-27.

[2] Cf. C. T. Davis, *Dante and the Idea of Rome*, (Oxford (1957). In the comparison of Langland and Dante contained in Pietro Calì's *Allegory and Vision in Dante and Langland*, Cork Univ. Press (1971), it seems to me that none of the serious underlying differences between the poets is adequately discussed much less analyzed.

[3] Cf. C. S. Lewis's review of A. M. F. Gunn's *The Mirror of Love*, *MÆ* XXII (1953), pp. 27 ff.

[4] Cf. R. Tuve, *Allegorical Imagery*, Princeton (1966), pp. 243 ff.

[5] Quoted by Janet Coleman, *Langland and the Moderni*, Rome (1981), p. 154.

[6] It may be that Langland's interest in grammatical 'comparison' was stimulated by the appearance of separate Latin treatises on *Comparacio* in the fourteenth century. English 'translations' and 'versions' appear to date from somewhat later in the fifteenth century. Cf. D. Thomson, *A Descriptive Catalogue of Middle English Grammatical Texts*, New York and London (1979), pp. 10-11, 51-2, 62-71.

[7] Compare the collection of proverbs and riddles in Rylands Lat. MS. 394, ed. by W. A. Panton, *Bulletin of the John Rylands Library*, 14 (1930); Peter Comester's *Historia Scholastica* (quoted at least twice by Langland); the *Ecloga Theoduli*. See also N. Orme, *English Schools in the Middle Ages*, London (1973); D. Thomson, *op. cit.*; D. Thomson, *A Study of the Middle English Treatises on Grammar*, Oxford D.Phil. thesis (1977).

[8] *The Allegory of Love*, Oxford (1936), p. 161. By the end of his life, Lewis had not changed his mind. See *'De Audiendis Poetis'* (*Medieval and Renaissance Literature*, ed. W. Hooper, Cambridge (1966), p. 9: 'From the premise that *Piers Plowman* is a great sermon, I think some have wrongly drawn the conclusion that it is a great poem. (That it contains great poetry, no one doubts; that is a distinct proposition.)'

INDEX